BEARDS & BALDNESS
IN THE
MIDDLE AGES

Translation, introduction & notes
by
Joseph McAlhany

LEVERHILL
BROOKLYN, NY

ISBN: 979-8-9896993-0-8
Library of Congress Control Number: 2023952360

Published by Leverhill
155 Water Street P 4/29
Brooklyn, NY 11201

Front cover images: *Top*: St. Benedict delivering his Rule to St. Maurus from a copy of the Rule at the monastery of St. Giles (Add. 16979, 21v). *Bottom*: Dagobert cutting off the beard of his tutor, from the 14th c. *Grandes Chroniques de France* (Royal MS 16 G VI, 93v). Both images are in the public domain thanks to the British Library.

Back cover image: A corbel dating from the 12th c. AD with two beard-pulling acrobats, part of the Metropolitan Museum of Arts collection located at The Cloisters.

BEARDS & BALDNESS IN THE MIDDLE AGES

THREE TEXTS

Synesius of Cyrene, *In Praise of Baldness*

Hucbald of Saint-Amand, *On Bald Men*

Burchard of Bellevaux, *A Defense of Beards*

INTRODUCTION

Hair and beards have a long tradition of symbolic associations, beginning with the first stirrings of civilization in ancient Mesopotamia and Egypt and continuing up to the present day. The presence or absence of hair, whether on the head, face, or body, has served to define the boundary between adulthood and immaturity, religious purity and worldliness, manliness and effeminacy, power and weakness, and civilization and barbarism. In various cultures around the world, rituals and ceremonies involving the cutting of hair or shaving mark important transitions in a human life, including its end, and first haircuts are still often treated as an important moment in a child's life. Hair thus serves in complex ways as a marker of identity, sometimes even standing in for a person as whole: a lock of hair, for example, as a token of love or remembrance.

The distinctions created by hair, as the partial list of polarities indicates, were never neutral. Implicitly or explicitly, hair in its various forms, including its absence, not only affirmed difference, but also confirmed beliefs of superiority or inferiority. These beliefs often rested upon which state was believed to be "natural," and it is no accident that the growth and loss of hair were frequently described with imagery drawn from the natural world, with comparisons to plants and animals. However, "natural" was a term, open to interpretation. It could be normative, describing the ways things ought to be, and "unnatural" deviations from the norm signaled corruption, decay, and perversity; its other antonym, "artificial," suggested something false and deceitful. On the other hand, "natural" could be simply descriptive, the way everything is—nothing is, in this view, "unnatural" and the "artificial" is the civilizing work of human hands to tame (or improve) wild and brutish nature. Views about the proper place of humans in this natural order, somewhere between beasts and gods in Aristotle's formulation, provided the basis for beliefs about hair.

For most of its history, the discussion of hair almost exclusively concerned men, and not only because writings on the topic were exclusively by men. According to the long-held view of the "natural order," women did not become bald or grow beards, and they were thus often excluded from the discussion (though Burchard's *A Defense of Beards* discusses the case of a bearded woman). Yet even when beards and hair were recognized as important markers of masculinity, there was never a single valued assigned to any particular form of them. Baldness, for example, could be a special marker of holiness or an indicator of a loss of virility; a smooth chin was to some evidence of urban sophistication, but to others proof of softness and decadence; gray hair might be a sign of maturity and wisdom, but could also signal a decline in vitality, the first hints of mortality. (Some of these beliefs remain prevalent today, at least to judge from the continued success of marketing hair-restoration solutions to men and hair-dyes to everyone.)

Since "natural" could also have moral connotations, hair was often seen not only as a manifestation of a man's biological vitality, but also as evidence of his moral fitness, especially in the case of beards. Men "naturally" grew beards, and thus the absence of one could suggest an "unnatural" effeminacy and moral corruption. "Beardless" was a woman's natural state, and thus evidence of a "natural" inferiority, but it was also a common descriptor of adolescent males who had not yet reached manhood, often carrying the insinuation of sexual desirability. A beardless adult male was morally suspect—unless, of course, the absence of a beard expressed a man's special status as a religious figure. In either case, the lack of a beard was something that was neither "normal" nor "natural." Baldness, however, complicated the discourse, since some men seemed to naturally grow bald, but while in general viewed negatively, it was also argued, though not always seriously, that it represented the perfection of a man's nature.

Conflicting views about beards and baldness are evident in their first appearances in art and literature. In ancient Sumeria, for example, priests shaved both their beards and their heads to indicate their special connection to the divine, separate from other mortals, while rulers represented themselves as both bearded and unbearded, in each case with a specific purpose: the bearded image emphasized their physical prowess in battle, while the clean-shaven look demonstrated their religious purity and divine status. In ancient Egypt nobles favored a clean-shaven look, but pharaohs often sported artificial beards of exaggerated length (the straps are often visible in artwork). The ambivalent values attributed to hair and beards persisted through the centuries: clerics in medieval Europe were expected to have short hair and shave their beards, but the holiest of men, hermits and ascetics, were known for their long hair and beards.

And as all fashions change over time, so did practices and beliefs about hair and beards. Early Greeks, for example, favored beards and considered beardlessness a sign of youth and effeminacy, but in the fourth century BC Alexander the Great promoted his image as a beardless young man, apparently to associate himself with the immortal youth of Apollo. During Rome's rise to the predominant power in the Mediterranean, from the second century BC to the first century AD, long hair and bushy beards marked out the barbarians of northern Europe. Romans, however, did not begin to shave regularly until the late third or early second century BC, when barbers were imported from the Greek cities of Sicily. Most elite Romans at this time maintained a close shave and hair of no great length, and Publius Cornelius Scipio Africanus Aemilianus, the conqueror of Rome's nemesis Carthage in 146 BC known for his admiration of Greek culture, adopted the smooth look of Alexander the Great. But in the second century AD, the emperor Hadrian made the full beard associated with philosophers (sometimes called the "philosopher's beard") fashionable, and statues of the emperor Marcus Aurelius, best known for his *Meditations*, present him with a full beard to symbolize his philosophical bent. Baldness, however, never seemed to lose its negative connotations. Julius Caesar, according to the biographer Suetonius, was sensitive about his thinning hair, and not only sported a comb-over but wore his triumphal garland as often as he could to disguise his baldness. Over a century later, the cruel emperor Domitian wrote a treatise on hair-care and dedicated it to a balding friend, encouraging him to bear the loss of his hair with courage.

In medieval Christianity, views about hair and beards, like much of medieval culture as a whole, were rooted in classical Greece and Rome but incorporated beliefs and practices derived from biblical texts and other Christian writing, particularly the lives of saints.[1] Moreover, these views about beards and beardlessness underwent some of the same shifts as in the earlier non-Christian world. For example, while the modern world has long been accustomed to portraits of a bearded Jesus, during the first five centuries of Christianity Jesus was just as likely to be represented beardless. But even as clerical regulations about beards and the tonsure came to be codified and the boundaries created by hair and its absence seemed to harden, there was never a consistency of meaning attributed to the presence or absence of hair and beards, either in the church or the secular world. There was the same variation and inconsistency in theory and practice as there had always been, and not only in the large-scale differences between eastern and western forms of Christianity, but even within the same local contexts and among individuals of the same social status.

Biblical texts provided justification for shaving as a ritual of purification and devotion to God, particularly the Levites and Nazarites of the Old Testament,[2] but for medieval Christianity, clerical regulations about hair originated in Paul's admonition against men growing their hair long at 1 Corinthians 11:14. In the King James version:

> Doth not even nature itself teach you, that, if a man have long hair,
> it is a shame unto him?[3]

As a result, during the first centuries of Christianity, clergy kept their hair short. The origins of monastic tonsure, perhaps the most distinctive form of hair associated with the Middle Ages, are obscure and controversial, but it seems to first appear among the priests of Gaul (modern-day France) in the sixth century AD and soon became a regular practice among clergy and monks.

And though there was not a specific prohibition against beards for clergy, shaving the beard became a requirement by the sixth century, helping to distinguish not only clergy from laymen, but also Christians from non-Christians and, in particular, Jews and Muslims. The earliest surviving rule about clerical beards dates from the fifth century, and in a rather amusing way demonstrates the vagaries of the evidence for the practice of shaving.[4] Canon 25 of the *Statuta ecclesiae antiqua* ("Early church regulations") reads:

> *clericus nec comam nutriat nec barbam radat.*
> A cleric should not grow his hair or shave his beard.

However, in order to bring the canon in line with what was the current practice about the beards of the religious, with the change of a single word the canon became:

> *clericus nec comam nutriat **sed** barbam radat.*
> A cleric should not grow his hair, **but** shave his beard.

In some cases, the final word was simply dropped:

> *clericus nec comam nutriat nec barbam ~~radat~~.*
> A cleric should not grow his hair or ~~shave~~ his beard.

Despite the regulation and expectation of shaving among clergy, the issue was still debated in the sixteenth century, when J.P. Valerian wrote *Pro sacerdotum barbis* ("On behalf of priests' beards"), exposing the alteration to the text of the original canon. Nonetheless, the requirement to shave survived until 1917, when it was finally dropped. It should be pointed out that shaving was not usually as close as it is today, resulting in smooth skin. Among the various monastic rules, shaving was never required more than once every two weeks, and in some cases it was closer to once a month, so many "beardless" monks must have frequently had short beards or at least some scruff.

Though different styles of hair and beards went in and out of fashion over the course of history, they were always weighted with meaning in whatever form they took. However, the evidence presents numerous interpretive pitfalls, and any general statements must be treated with caution. Any particular text on the subject may represent an individual and idiosyncratic perspective, not necessarily reflecting widely shared views. Moreover, images of individuals are often symbolic and idealized rather than real, which was as true for portraits in illuminated manuscripts of the Middle Ages as for the statues of ancient Mesopotamia and Egypt. The emperor Charlemagne (748-814 AD), for example, was portrayed both with and without a beard, and his grandson, Charles the Bald, is pictured with hair, though literary sources, including Hucbald's poem translated below, suggest he was in fact bald.

Each of the three texts presented here, from different places and times during the Middle Ages, reflect the inconsistencies, complexities, and anxieties surrounding the social and cultural meanings assigned to beards and baldness. Ranging from a fifth-century Greek-speaking intellectual in Egypt to a twelfth-century Cistercian abbot in Latin Europe, the authors presented here speak of beards and baldness in quite different ways, though all display a healthy sense of humor about the topic. Each of them, as idiosyncratic as they may be, enrich our understanding of beards and baldness in the Middle Ages, and each in its own right is a valuable contribution to the literature and intellectual history of the worlds from which they emerged.

Synesius of Cyrene

Synesius was born around 370 AD to a wealthy and noble family of Cyrene, located on the north coast of Africa in modern-day Libya. In his youth, he received a solid education in the classical tradition, as is clear from his wide-ranging writings, and sometime after 390 he went to Alexandria, the great cultural center of the Mediterranean world, where he studied under the famous philosopher and mathematician Hypatia. In a letter shortly after hearing her lecture for the first time, he called her "the true guide to the mysteries of philosophy," and later, near the end of his life, he addressed her in a farewell letter as "mother, sister, teacher, and in all these forms my benefactor."[5] In the fall of 397, he put his studies on hold and travelled to the imperial capital Constantinople on a diplomatic mission to seek tax relief on behalf of the five cities of western Cyrene known collectively as Pentapolis (Greek for "five cities," which were Cyrene, Berenice, Ptolemais, Apollonia, and Arsinoe). During his time there, he composed *De regno* ("On kingship"), in the form of an address to the emperor Arcadius criticizing the reliance on "barbarians" such as Goths to supply troops, and *De providentia* ("On providence"), also known as *Egyptians* or *Egyptian Tales*, a political allegory of a palace coup based on Egyptian mythology.

He returned to his native city in 401, where he was baptized. There has been some dispute as to whether he was born a Christian or converted later, but most likely he was raised as a Christian, though not an orthodox one (what "Christian" meant varied as much then as it does today). In any case, he was a serious thinker well-versed in both Christian and Neoplatonic traditions. The following year he visited Alexandria again, where he married a Christian wife in a ceremony officiated by Theophilus, the patriarch of Alexandria. After a couple of years, he once again returned to Cyrene, devoting himself to literary pursuits, but also taking an active role in organizing the defenses against the frequent attacks of nomadic tribes from the south. By this time he was father to three boys, including twins. In 410, Theophilus offered Synesius the bishopric of Ptolemais. Despite some reservations more practical than theological, he accepted the office and soon found himself involved in political conflicts, including with Andronicus, the governor of Cyrenaica, whom Synesius eventually excommunicated. He likely also visited Athens before he was consecrated as bishop. In 412, Synesius lost all three of his young sons and died shortly afterwards.

In addition to *In Praise of Baldness* and the two works mentioned above, he also wrote *De insomniis*, a treatise on dreams; *Cynegetica*, a work on hunting; *Dion*, a treatise addressed to a son not yet born and named for Dio Chrysostom, the philosopher and rhetorician whose speech in praise of hair led to *In Praise of Baldness*; nine hymns representing a mixture of Neoplatonism and Christianity; and a collection of 156 letters, several of which are addressed to Hypatia.

In Praise of Baldness
Bearing the title Φαλάκρας Ἐγκώμιον but often referred to by the Lat-

in title *Encomium calvitiae, In Praise of Baldness* is a playful and learned treatise, much in the manner of the rhetorical exercises in which elite young men were educated. It is not known at what point he composed it, and scholars argue for wildly different dates: no later than 399, positively after 411, or some other date in between. In one of his letters (74), Synesius claims the encomium is the result of exacting labor but disavows any claim that it is to be taken seriously. It is certainly a showpiece of literary refinement and scholarship, filled with word-play, rhetorical devices, recherché vocabulary, and references to the philosophy, history, and literature of classical Greece.

The text begins with reference to a speech in praise of hair by Dio Chrysostom, a renowned first century AD orator and philosopher, which has been lost and is known only through Synesius' quotations. Synesius, who playfully confesses to his emotional struggles as he started to go bald, claims Dio's clever speech stimulated him to offer a rebuttal and rise to the defense of baldness. In a *tour de force* of ironic erudition, he counters Dio's arguments with his own examples, drawn from literary sources (Homer in particular) as well as the world around him, and elevates baldness into something divine.

There have been a number of editions and translations into various languages, the most recent of which is by Lamoureux and Aujoulat (2004) as part of the Budé series of Greek and Latin texts (their text serves as the basis of the translation here). An English translation was produced by Augustine Fitzgerald in 1930, which remains serviceable, while the more recent translation by Alcock (2018), available online, has its moments, but is rife with inaccuracies.

Hucbald of Saint-Amand

Born sometime between 840 and 850, Hucbald seems to have been related to Carolingian royalty on his mother's side. He was raised in the abbey of Saint-Amand (formerly Elnon), located on the modern-day border between France and Belgium, likely as an oblate. There Hucbald studied under Milo, poet and school-master of Saint-Amand, sometimes said to be Hucbald's uncle. At some point Hucbald left Saint-Amand

and, alongside Remigius of Auxerre, who would go on to become one of the most prolific authors of his age, became a student of the Benedictine scholar Heiric of Auxerre. (According to one tradition, Hucbald left Saint-Amand to avoid becoming a rival to Milo for leadership of the school.) When Milo died in 872, Hucbald returned to Saint-Amand to succeed him, but by 883, when the abbey Saint-Amand was destroyed by the Normans, he was teaching at the abbey of Saint Bertin (Sithiu) in Saint-Omer at the northern tip of France. According to one source, he opened a school at Nevers at the request of the bishop, and when he later left, was allowed by the bishop to take a souvenir. He took relics of the child Saint Cyricus with him back to Saint-Amand, where they remain to this day. In 893, Fulco, the archbishop who succeeded Hincmar at Rheims and former abbot of Saint-Bertin, invited Hucbald and Remigius to teach there in an attempt to restore the reputation it once had for learning. Their combined efforts brought back the luster to the school of Rheims, which had been destroyed during the Norman invasions. When Fulco was killed in 900, it seems likely Hucbald again returned to Saint-Amand.

Hucbald died on June 20, 930, perhaps after reaching the ripe old age of 90. Upon his death, eighteen of his books were donated to Saint-Amand, including works by Plato (the *Timaeus* in the Latin translation by the fourth-century thinker Chalcidius), Seneca, Vergil, and Eutropius. He was buried in the same tomb as Milo, and his epitaph alludes not only to his musical and hagiographical works, but also to his translation of Saint Cyricus' relics from Nevers to Saint-Amand:

> *dormit in hac tumba simplex sine felle columba*
> *doctor flos et honos tam cleri quam monachorum*
> *Hucbaldus fama<m> cuius per climata mundi*
> *edita sanctorum modulamina gestaque clamant.*
> *hic Cyrici membra pretiosa reperta Nivernis*
> *nostris invexit oris scripsitque triumphum.*

> In this tomb sleeps a simple and peaceable dove,
> a scholar, flower and honor of clergy as well as monks,
> Hucbald, whose fame the melodic scales and lives of the saints

sent through the world's regions proclaim.
The precious limbs of Cyr, discovered in Nevers,
he brought to our lands and wrote of his triumph.

Among the saints whose lives he wrote are Saint Rictrude, the first abottess of Marchiennes, and Saint Aldegundis, founder and first abbess of Maubeuge Abbey in Hennegau. He also wrote an account of the martyrdom of Saint Cyricus and his mother Julitta, and dedicated two hymns to Saint Theodoricus, patron of the cloister of Mont d'Hor near Rheims. However, Hucbald may be best known for his work on music, particularly the *Harmonica institutio* ("Treatise on Harmony"), which relies heavily upon Martianus Capella and Boethius. A *Musica enchiridis* ("Handbook on Music") was falsely attributed to him. Other works reveal a broad range of intellectual interests: a poem on the Egyptian days (for which he used a poem found in the *Latin Anthology*), a poem *De sobrietate* ("On Moderation") dedicated in 876 to Charles the Bald, and the poem translated here, the *De calvis* ("On Bald Men").

On Bald Men

Dedicated to Hatto, the archbishop of Mainz,[6] Hucbald's poem on bald men is found in several manuscripts from the tenth to twelfth centuries. There have been three editions, all dating from the latter half of the nineteenth century, the most recent of which, by von Winterfeld (1899), is the basis for the translation here.[7] *On Bald Men* begins with 54 hexameters addressed to Hatto, the archbishop of Mainz, in which Hucbald gives examples, drawn from Macrobius' *Saturnalia*, of poets receiving rewards for their efforts. He also explains in this prefatory section that the poem proper, which carries the title *Ecloga de calvis* ("A short poem on bald men"), will consist of 136 verses in which every word begins with C, the first letter of the Latin word for bald (*calvus*). After three introductory lines, there are thirteen sections of ten lines each, followed by a conclusion of three lines. (The sections were given descriptive headings, but these are not by Hucbald.) After an initial section acknowledging the favor God has bestowed upon the bald, the next five sections praise the bald according to various occupations in which they can be found, including abbots and monks, grammarians and poets, kings and commanders, and medical doctors. Hucbald then responds to those who criticize baldness, after which two sections turn to the biblical examples of Elijah and Paul. He concludes with a warning to an unnamed individual and speaks of someone struck blind for criticism of the Carolingian emperor Charles the Bald. One additional section, which is found only in some manuscripts and brings the total to 146 rather than the 136 specified, is not by Hucbald but has been translated here.

As noted, the most notable feature of *On Bald Men* is that each and every word begins with the letter C, which places an enormous strain on sense and syntax. Somewhat foolishly, I have attempted to replicate the unremitting alliteration, in part because it forces the translation into the same awkward vocabulary and phrasing as the original. Desilve's nineteenth-century translation into French is a serviceable trot. There is also a delightful English translation by Klein (1995), who took a different approach to the thankless task, including the inspired adoption of "Kojak" as a term for a bald man, though the significance of the name will likely be lost on readers not alive in the 1970s.

BURCHARD OF BELLEVAUX (BEAUVAIS)

Aside from his death in 1163 (or 1165), little is known about Burchard. His name suggests a Germanic origin, but there can be no certainty about his family background or his origins. He was a Cistercian monk and devoted follower of Saint Bernard, famed monastic reformer and founder of the abbey of Clairvaux in 1115. Given what is known of his career, he was likely born around 1100, a decade or so after Bernard. There is no mention of Burchard in any cartularies (collections of records) of Clairvaux prior to 1136, when he became the first abbot of Balerne, a Benedictine monastery located near France's modern border with Switzerland that had become Cistercian by the time of Burchard's appointment. A bull of Innocent II from 1138, which survives second-hand, notes that Burchard was accepted as abbot of Balerne after he was received from Clairvaux, in accordance with the wishes (*votis*) of its monks.[8] He remained there over twenty years, and then in 1159 became the second abbot of Bellevaux, founded around 1117 roughly sixty miles to the north of Balerne. He died a few years later.

His close relationship to Bernard is attested by a letter from Bernard to Burchard as abbot of Balerne in response to some queries. The response is too vague to determine what these were, but Bernard begins by noting Burchard's "fiery" language and ends with mention of a future visit.[9] Aside from *A Defense of Beards*, only two small samples of his writing survive. One is a brief postscript to William of Saint-Thierry's life of Bernard after William's death in 1148,[10] in which he touts William's suitability for writing Bernard's life. The other is a letter to Nicholas of Clairvaux, who became Bernard's secretary. He opens the letter with an ironic appeal to Nicholas to accept Burchard's simple style: "How can a turtle address a winged bird? How can a mole leap with the stag? How can a cricket trumpet to the swan's melody?" Although brief, the letter demonstrates some of the same playful spirit and linguistic exuberance found in *A Defense of Beards*.

A Defense of Beards

This work was unknown less than a century ago, coming to light in 1929 when E.P. Goldschmidt discovered the manuscript at a Swiss bookseller's. It is a copy, not in Burchard's own hand, with a few additions and some alterations, including a sketch of nine types of beard. Goldschmidt sold the manuscript to the British Museum, with the provision that he be allowed to produce the first edition, which he did in a limited run of 350 copies in 1935.[11] In 1985, R.B.C Huygens produced a critical edition in the series *Corpus Chrisianorum*, with valuable notes on the copious references and allusions to biblical passages as well as other Christian texts, and this has been used for the translation. (Huygens' edition is preceded by a lengthy introduction to hair and beards in the Middle Ages by Giles Constable, which is the best and most thorough treatment of the subject.)

As the only known text devoted to beards between the emperor Julian's *Misopogon* ("The Beard-hater") in 353 AD and the J.P. Valerian's *Pro sacerdotum barbis* ("On behalf of priests' beards") in 1531, Burchard's

Apologia is of particular importance to studies of hair, but it is also a notable as a piece of medieval literature in its own right. Aside from providing another example of biblical exegesis and evidence for the status of lay-brothers, it is a remarkable mixture of playfulness and pedantry that reflects major currents in twelfth century thought and brings to light a lively and idiosyncratic medieval intellectual. There is, to my knowledge, no complete translation in English or any other language.

Addressed to the lay-brothers at Rosières, a monastery thirty miles southwest of Bellevaux in the same diocese of Besançon, *A Defense of Beards* was apparently intended to quell unrest following a misunderstanding about a letter or some other piece of writing of Burchard's. Our only information about it and the unrest it created comes from the *Apologia* itself, but it seems the lay-brothers (*conversi*) believed they were being compelled to shave their beards. (In the Cistercian order, monks were clean-shaven, but lay-brothers were allowed to have beards.) The exact nature and status of lay-brothers is unclear and seemed to vary depending on time and place, but in general they were individuals who entered monasteries as adults and whose primary function was to provide agricultural labor. Since they were not ordained, they were not subject to the same regulations as clergy and monks, and as *A Defense of Beards* amply demonstrates, they were often considered to be uneducated and of an inferior status (they have been called "second-class monks"). As a result, tensions between lay-brothers and monks often ran high, and there were numerous incidents of protest, which on occasion turned violent.

Burchard attempts to alleviate the lay-brothers' concern about their beards, since, as he claims, it was based on a misunderstanding of what he had written. The defense, however, goes far beyond clarifying the confusion, and over the course of three separate sermons, Burchard discourses not only over the types and nature of beards, but he also supplies numerous examples of allegorical readings of biblical passages concerned with beards. And although the title refers only to beards, Burchard also discusses hair and baldness, with special attention to the tonsure. Beards had been given allegorical treatment before Burchard, notably by the great sixth-century scholar Cassiodorus and Rabanus Maurus, the ninth-century archbishop of Mainz and prolific author. Augustine, in a commentary on Psalm 33 (34), discussed the saliva flowing onto David's beard to which Burchard devotes several chapters in the first sermon. In fact, there are a few sections in *A Defense of Beards* heavily dependent on Rabanus or freely cribbed from Augustine as well as Bede, yet the vast majority of it reveals the author's lively mind.

The first sermon, on the cleanliness of beards, presents a list of three types of vermin that can infest beards and associates these three vermin with specific vices. Burchard turns to an allegorical interpretation of Aaron's beard from Psalm 132 (133):2, a text also used by Rabanus Maurus and Augustine, to promote the spiritual cleansing of the lay-brothers' "inner beards." Burchard also provides allegorical interpretations of the leprous beard in Leviticus and David's saliva-covered beard when he feigns madness before king Achish. The second sermon, on the styling and form of beards, begins with an amusing catalog of various types of beards and moustaches, and then engages in allegorical interpretation of the beards of David's messengers that were shaved in half and the more complex case of Ezekiel's beard. In elucidating the distinctions between lay-brothers and monks, Burchard also introduces the question of the tonsure.

The third sermon, equal in length to the first two combined. is on the nature of the beard, and along with further biblical exegesis, discusses the different types of beards in terms of their moral significance (based in part on beards as a marker of sex, which leads to discussion of the bearded woman Galla). He also discusses the beard as a sign of five different virtues and concludes with some lengthy analysis about the distinction between monks and lay-brothers in shaving and tonsure. In addition to exegesis of Mephiboseth from 2 Samuel, Burchard also provides a detailed interpretation of two adolescents described as part of a vision by a desert hermit. He concludes with the question of the status of beards and hair after the resurrection. At points in his sermons, Burchard deploys technical vocabulary and logical frameworks, at times as tedious as they are thorough, and it is difficult to determine if these sections are to be taken in all seriousness. Certainly the lay-brothers would not have found them persuasive, or even intelligible.

Notes

1. For an overview, see Roberta Milliken's introduction to *A Cultural History of Hair in the Middle Ages* (London and New York: Bloomsbury, 2019), 1-17. Neither Synesius nor Burchard are mentioned in this volume, and Hucbald is mentioned only once in passing. See also R. Bartlett, "Symbolic Meanings of Hair in the Middle Ages" (*Transactions of the Royal Historical Society* 4:43-60, 1994) and Constable (1985).

2. See Numbers 6:5, Leviticus 19:27, 21:5.

3. The next verse addresses women's hair: "But if a woman have long hair, it is a glory to her: for her hair is given her for a covering."

4. See Constable (1985) 103-6.

5. *Ep.* 137.8-9: τῆς γνησίας καθηγεμόνος τῶν φιλοσοφίας ὀργίων; 16.2-3: μῆτερ καὶ ἀδελφὴ καὶ διδάσκαλε καὶ διὰ πάντων τούτων εὐεργετική.

6. Hanno was educated by Alcuin and after succeeding abbot Rabanus at Fulda, became archbishop of Mainz (Moguntinus).

7. See von Winterfeld (1899) 262-64.

8. See Chauvin (1989) 43.

9. Letter 146, which concludes: *necessitates tuas ut meas portabo, cum venero* ("I will treat your needs as my own when I arrive.) See J. Leclercq and H. Rochais, eds. *Sancti Bernardi opera. Vol. 7, Epistolae I. Corpus epistolarum 1-180* (Rome: Editiones Cistercienses, 1974); Letter 152 in B.S. James, *The Letters of St. Bernard of Clairvaux* (Kalamazoo, MI: Cistercian Publications, repr. 1998).

10. See P. Verdeyen and C. Van de Viere, eds. *Vita prima sancti Bernardi Claraevallis abbatis: Liber primus* (Turnout: Brepols, 2011).

11. My chance discovery of one of these in a used bookstore in Portland, Oregon led to this translation.

BIBLIOGRAPHY

Synesius of Cyrene

Bregman, J. *Synesius of Cyrene: Philosopher-Bishop.* Berkeley: University of California Press, 1982.

—. "Synesius of Cyrene." *The Cambridge History of Philosophy in Late Antiquity.* L. P. Gerson, ed. Cambridge: Cambridge University Press, 2010. 520-37.

Cameron, A. and J. Long. *Barbarians and Politics at the Court of Arcadius.* Berkeley: University of California Press, 1993.

Druon, E. *Études sur la vie et les oeuvres de Synesius.* Paris: Auguste Durans, 1859. 250-60.

Kennedy, G. A. Greek Rhetoric under Christian Emperors. Princeton, NJ: Princeton University Press, 1983. 35-45.

Roques, D. *Synésios de Cyrène et la Cyrénaïque du Bas-Empire.* Paris: CNRS, 1987.

Editions & Translations

Alcock, A. *Synesius, Encomium Calvitii.* https://www.roger-pearse.com/weblog/2018/09/22/a-new-translation-of-synesius-encomium-of-calvitius-from-anthony-alcock. 2018.

Fitzgerald. A. *The Essays and Hymns of Synesius of Cyrene.* Vol 2. Oxford: Oxford University Press, 1930.

Garzya, A. *Sinesio. Opere, epistole, operette, inni.* Turin: Unione Tipografico-Editrice Torinese, 1989. (= Terzaghi 1944).

Lamoureaux, J. and N. Aujoulat. *Synésios de Cyrène. Tome IV: Opuscules I.* Paris: Les Belles Lettres, 2004.

Romero, F. A. G. *Sinesio De Cirene. Himnos, Tratados.* Madrid: Editorial Gredos, 1993. (= Terzaghi 1944).

Terzaghi, N. *Synesii Cyrenensis opuscula.* Rome: Polygraphica, 1944.

Hucbald of Saint Amand

Chartier, Y. *L'oeuvre musicale d'Hucbald de Saint-Amand: les compositions et le traité de musique.* Saint-Laurent (Québec): Éditions Bellarmin, 1995.

—. "Clavis Operum Hucbaldi Elnonensis: Bibliographie des oeuvres d'Hucbald de Saint-Amand." *JML* 5 (1995): 202-24.

Desilve, J. *De schola Elnonensi Sancti Amandi a saeculo IX ad XII usque.* Louvain: Carolus Peeters, 1890.

Leclercq, H. "Hucbald." *Dictionnaire d'archéologie chrétienne et de liturgie,* vol. 6.2. F. Cabrol and H. Leclercq, eds. Paris: Librairie Letouzey et Ané,

1925. 2772-76.

Manitius, M. *Geschichte der Lateinischen Literatur des Mittelalters.* 3 vols. Munich: C.H. Beck, 1911. 1.588-94.

Raby, F. J. E. *A History of Secular Latin Poetry.* 2nd ed. 2 vols. Oxford: Oxford University Press, 1957. 2:249.

van der Essen, L. "Hucbald de Saint-Amand (840-930) et sa place dans le mouvement hagiographique médiéval." *Revue d'histoire ecclésiastique* 19 (1923): 333-55, 522-52.

Weakland, R. "Hucbald as musician and theorist." *The Musical Quarterly* 52 (1956): 66-84.

Editions & Translations

Corpet, E. *Hucbaldi Elnonensis monachi de laude calvorum carmen mirabile.* Paris: Pommeret et Moreau, 1853.

Desilve, I. *Hucbaldi Elnonensis Monachi De laude calvorum carmen mirabile. Le poëme admirable d'Hucbald moine de Saint-Amand à la louange des chauves.* Valenciennes: G. Giard et Seulin, 1875.

Klein, T. "In Praise of Bald Men: A Translation of Hucbald's *Ecloga de Calvis*." *Comitatus* 26: 1-9 (1995).

Sandys, W. *Specimens of Macaronic Poetry.* London: Richard Beckley, 1931. 21-27.

von Barth, K. "Hugbaldi monachi Ecloga de laudibus calvitii." *Adversariorum commentariorum libri LX.* Frankfort am Main, 1624, 2175-77 (= Migne, *Patrologiae Latinae* 132.1041-104).

von Winterfeld, P. *Monumenta Germaniae Historica* 4.1. Berlin: Weidmann, 1899. 265-71.

BURCHARD OF BELLEVAUX

Chauvin, B. "Un disciple méconnu de Saint Bernard, Burchard, Abbé de Balerne puis de Bellevaux (Vers 1100-†1164)." *Cîteaux: Commentarii Cistercienses* 40 (1989): 5-68.

Constable, G. "Introduction." In R.B.C. Huygens, *Apologiae Duae.* Corpus Christianorum: Continuatio Mediaevalis 62. Turnhout: Brepols, 1985. 47-150.

—. "*famuli* and *conversi* at Cluny: A Note on Statute 24 of Peter the Venerable." In *The Abbey of Cluny: A Collection of Essays to Mark the Eleven-Hundredth Anniversary of its Foundation.* Berlin: Lit Verlag, 2010. 381-404.

Donnelly, J. S. *The Decline of the Medieval Cistercian Laybrotherhood.* New York: Fordham University Press, 1949.

France, J. *Separate but Equal: Cistercian Lay Brothers, 1120-1350*. Collegeville, Minnesota: Liturgical Press, 2012.

Hallinger, P. K. "Woher kommen die Laienbrüder?" *Analecta Sacri Ordinis Cisterciensis* 12 (1956): 1-104.

Hofmeister, P. "Der Streit um das Priesters Bart." *Zeitschrift für Kirchengeschichte* 62 (1943-44): 72-94.

Platelle, H. "Le problème de scandale: Les nouvelles modes masculines aux XIe et XIIe siècles." *Revue belge de philologie et d'histoire* 53 (1975): 1071-96.

Editions

Goldschmidt, E. *Burchardus de Bellevaux: Apologia de Barbis*. Cambridge: Cambridge University Press, 1935.

Huygens, R.B.C. *Apologiae Duae*. Corpus Christianorum: Continuatio Mediaevalis 62. Turnhout: Brepols, 1985.

SYNESIUS OF CYRENE
IN PRAISE OF BALDNESS

1. Golden-tongued Dio wrote a book,[1] a speech in praise of hair, and so brilliant was it that a bald man would have no choice but to feel shame in the face of his argument. Moreover, his argument has the support of nature, since it's in everyone's nature to desire to be beautiful, and hair, which nature created to be our companion from infancy, constitutes an important element of beauty. When, to my horror, my own hair began to fall out, I was pained to the depths of my heart. And it continued to fall: at first individual hairs tumbled one by one to the ground, then they fell two at a time, and finally entire clumps. A battle raged as my head was plundered and ravaged—at the time I believed my suffering was worse than the Athenians' when Archidamus cut down the Acharnians' olive groves.[2] Before long I looked like one of those hapless Euboeans from Homer's epic, sent to the war against Troy with *locks flowing behind*.[3] Was there any god or any demon I didn't blame at that time? I even started to write a work in praise of Epicurus, not because I agreed with him about the gods, but because I wanted to get back at them as much as I could.[4] Where is Providence to be found, I would ask, when everyone gets the opposite of what they deserve? What did I do wrong to end up looking so repellent to women? It wouldn't be such a serious matter if it was only my neighbors' wives, since when it comes to Aphrodite's business, I'm as virtuous as can be—I could rival Bellerophon himself for self-control.[5]

But they say even mothers and sisters take an interest in the beauty of the men in their family, as Parysatis made clear when she rejected the regal Artaxerxes for the handsome Cyrus.[6]

2. And so I bewailed my condition and contemplated taking drastic measures to remedy my misfortune, but over time I got used to it. Reason then arrived to take up the struggle against my suffering, which retreated little by little until it became easier to bear and I recovered. But now it's Dio himself who responds with another torrent of words, and he's renewed the attack against me with the assistance of an advocate.[7] "Against two, not even Heracles could" goes the saying, since he couldn't withstand the two sons of Molione when they ambushed him.[8] Likewise, in his struggle against the Hydra, he fought the monster one-on-one for a good while, but when the crab came to the Hydra's aid, Heracles would've given up if he hadn't brought in Iolaos as an ally.[9] It seems like much the same thing is happening to me at Dio's hands, but I don't have an Iolaos for a nephew. As a result, I once again forgot myself and all my rational arguments, and now compose an elegy—a funeral dirge for my hair.

"But you're the best of the bald," I say to myself, "and you seem to possess a noble character, giving not a thought to your misfortune. In fact, when everybody's looks undergo scrutiny as the pea-soup is served, you select yourself as your target, as if you took pride in your baldness, like it was something good.[10] Certainly you can endure Dio's speech, and keep 'your heart under control,' as they say, just like Odysseus remained unmoved when confronted by the wanton behavior of his female servants.[11] You too should resist feeling mistreated by anyone. What do you mean you can't? Certainly you can! Just listen—there's no need to unroll the scroll and read it. I'll recite it for you since there aren't many lines to it. It's a nicely polished piece, in fact, and its charm sticks in your memory. I couldn't forget it even if I wanted to."

Dio's Speech

3. "After waking up at dawn and praying to the gods, just as I always do, I tended to my hair. For quite some time I had neglected it, as I'd been feeling quite unwell. Much of it, in fact, had become matted and tangled, like the wool that hangs from the legs of sheep, but much stiffer, as if it had been woven out of very fine strands. In short, my hair was wild-looking and unwieldy, and as I was trying with some difficulty to untangle it, much of it was torn off or pulled out.

"It was then the idea came to me to compose something in praise of lovers of hair, those people who as lovers of beauty place great value on their hair and take no little pains in caring for it—they always carry a reed comb in their hair to straighten it whenever they have a spare moment. And, something that requires serious effort, they make sure their hair never touches the ground whenever they lie down to sleep, placing a small block of wood under their head to keep it as far from the ground as possible. They give more thought to keeping their hair neat than to sleeping soundly! Apparently it's their hair that makes them handsome and fearsome, but sleep, even if very sound, renders them sluggish and careless.

"It seems even the Spartans weren't negligent when it came to hair. Arriving before that great and terrible battle when they alone among the Greeks, three hundred in number, were going to face the King of Persia, they sat down and tended to their hair.[12] I believe Homer also thought it was something deserving a great deal of attention. Not often does he praise handsome men for their eyes, nor does he think these are a particularly beautiful feature. In fact, he doesn't praise the eyes of any hero except Agamemnon, and even then it's only along with rest of his body.[13] And he doesn't only call the Greeks 'quick-glancing'[14] (this epithet, common to all Greeks, applies equally to Agamemnon); he praises all of them for their hair, beginning with Achilles:

> she took hold of Peleus' son by his blond hair[15]

Then Menelaus receives the epithet *blond*[16] on account of his hair, and Homer mentions Hector's locks:

> his dark locks were tossed about[17]

When Euphorbus, the most beautiful of all the Trojans, died, there was no other lament than this:

> his hair wet with blood, hair like the Graces,

> *his braids which were clasped with gold and silver*[18]

And when he wanted to indicate Odysseus had been made handsome by Athena, he says:

> *his hairs darkened*[19]

And likewise:

> *down his head*
> *fell curly locks like the bloom of a hyacinth*[20]

Praise of hair is apparently more appropriate for men than for women, at least in Homer. In fact, he doesn't always mention hair when describing the beauty of women, and even in the case of the gods he praises females in other ways, such as *golden Aphrodite, ox-eyed Hera,* and *silver-footed Thetis.* But when it comes to Zeus, he lavishes praise on his hair: *the ambrosial locks of the lord flowed.*"[21]

4. Here you have Dio's own words. Now, since I'm not the worst at seeing the future, I was sure I'd see Thrasymachus blush, but no such thing has yet happened to me.[22] At first I was completely enthralled by his argument. Now, however, I think Dio is a clever speaker who doesn't have anything important to say, but still gives speeches because he has too much ability not to. In fact, he'd have earned far more admiration if he'd chosen to praise the opposite position, the one which my own head occupies. Imagine what he could have done as "a helper to the helpless"[23] if only he'd tackled a subject that would have allowed his abilities to shine! Instead, since he possesses hair as well as rhetorical skill, he applied his skill to his hair. And the way he inserted himself into his composition was quite clever: in his speech no one else but him is a lover of hair, no one else but him curls his coif with a comb made of reed—the same reed he used to compose his speech![24] But even if I'm bald, I still have some ability to make speeches, and though Dio might be more beautiful than me, my subject is even more beautiful than his. So why shouldn't I strip down for a fight and put myself and my argument to the test, to see if I can cover in shame those men still covered with hair? So I'll make a speech, but without a stately and polished opening of the type rhetoricians deploy

to arm their speeches for combat, like battle-rams on a ship. Nor will my speech open with a rhythmic and sonorous poetic prelude of the kind Dio composed in the manner of a harpist's melody:

> *After waking up at dawn and praying to the gods, just as I always do, I tended to my hair. For quite some time I had neglected it, as I had been feeling quite unwell.*

He continues on in this vein, recounting the evidence of his carelessness, until without our noticing it he leads us into praise of his carefulness. This is what those clever craftsmen of speeches do to us: one moment they charm us, the next they hoodwink us.

I probably understand things as well as anyone, but I don't spend any time on rhetoric. Instead, there are two arts that govern my life: growing a garden and raising the bravest hunting dogs. These fingers of mine are well-practiced with hoes and boar-spears, but not a reed—unless you mean the reed of an arrow-shaft instead of a writer's pen. Don't be shocked if my fingers are now wrapped around this kind of reed as well. But I won't dishonor my family's rustic way of life and make a show of well-rounded pretty little speeches with any preludes or prefaces. I'll take what I consider the best course, especially for a man from the country, and set out in plain view straightforward expressions of my thoughts. I'll fight using facts, only modulating my tone between conversational and argumentative, from the Dorian mode, as they say, to the Phrygian.[25] I'll run out of breath before getting to all the arguments that will, I'm sure, pour from my heart.

5. My speech will prove that a bald man is the last person who should feel ashamed. What does a bald scalp matter if the mind bristles, as the poet sang of Achilles?[26] He had no concern for his hair, and even offered it to a corpse![27] In fact, hairs are dead: non-living things attached to living beings. This is why animals that lack reason have hair covering their entire body, but a human, if he has enjoyed a life of some distinction, is almost entirely shorn of this burden we're born with. But to make sure he doesn't think too highly of himself and forget he shares in the common lot of mortal beings, hair still grows on his body in a few places. So anyone without hair even in these few places stands in the same relation to other humans as humans to beasts. And as humans are the most intelligent as well as the least hairy creatures on earth, sheep, as is well known, are the stupidest of all herd animals, which is why their hair grows in bunches, not in separate strands. The conclusion is that the presence of hair is antithetical to intelligence, since in no instance are they naturally disposed to co-exist. And if a contribution is required from hunters (men who are themselves as dear to me as the skill they possess), the cleverest dogs are the ones with bare ears and bellies.[28] Hairy ones are rash and over-bold, best kept away from the hunt.

And if wise Plato, when speaking of the team that drives the chariot of the soul, calls the unjust horse "hair-deaf" in regard to its ears,[29] how can he think there's anything good about hair? Even if Plato hadn't said it, anyone with hair growing over the place where our hearing is located must be deaf, just as anyone with hair growing over the place where our sight is located must be blind. What a monstrosity that would be if it actually happened! Twinned hairs already sprout on the eyelids, and it seems the utmost of evils when hairs become lodged in the eye. Every means, including violence, is brought to bear against them to prevent them from gouging the eye. In fact, nature can't tolerate the conjunction of what is most honorable with what is most dishonorable. The organs of sense perception are the most honorable parts of a living being, and of all the body parts they're the ones that make a living being truly alive. The soul distributes its powers to these parts first, and sight is not only the most divine of them all, but also the baldest. In addition, just as the most honorable parts of a single human are the baldest, the same relation holds true for the best of a species in relationship to the species as a whole (as was demonstrated just above). And within a single species, the further removed an individual is from hairiness, the further from beastliness. So if humans are the most divine of all animals, then among all humans the one who has the good fortune to shed his hair—a bald man—must be the most divine of all beings upon the earth.

6. Look at paintings in a museum,[30] the ones of Diogenes or Socrates or any other of those wise men from antiquity—it's like a theater of the bald! Don't let Apollonius[31] or any other sorcerer who's an expert in the supernatural create any confusion about my argument. They might dupe most people into believing they have hair, but in fact they don't. Maybe sorcerers don't even possess wisdom, but instead some kind of magical ability; not a kind of knowledge, but a power. For this reason, lawgivers regard wisdom as something deserving the greatest honor, but keep executioners around for the sorcerers. So even if Apollonius did have hair, it's irrelevant—I have friendly feelings for the man, and I would want him to be counted among the bald. On the basis of what I've already said, it's likely the converse of the argument holds true: if someone is wise, then he's bald, but if he isn't bald, then he's not wise.

When it comes to demonic matters, it's the same. You've been a spectator to the rites of Dionysus—the Bacchic revelers are covered with hair, some with their own, others with hair borrowed from another source (nothing is as Bacchic as a fawn-skin, and some even use pine branches for "hair"). One sees all of them leaping about and cavorting in their unruly prancing whenever, as it seems to me, they're overcome by strong drink (whatever strong drink it is that's part of their rituals). In any case, they seem to get carried away with some unnatural and outrageous behavior. Also included in these rituals are the seat and whip of Silenus,[32] who's represented as Dionysus' teacher. Since he's bald, I suppose he has to remain wise and self-controlled while among the frenzied crowd. Moreover, you shouldn't think it unimportant that Zeus honored him above all other demons when he chose him to be the attendant and tutor of his little boy. For Dionysus also has to drink the unmixed wine and sometimes succumbs to the mania of natural desires, reaching such a point of derangement that he dances together with the Bacchic revelers. But Silenus moderates Dionysus' madness to prevent him from going too far without realizing it and becoming too troublesome for his father to manage.

Now that we have sufficient evidence, we need to return to our point that brains are present where hairs are absent and hairs present where brains are absent. This is why even Socrates, son of Sophroniscus, moderate in all other respects and more than anyone else reluctant to accept praise of his own qualities, was unable to refrain from taking pride in his likeness to Silenus: to make his head a receptacle of intelligence was all he wanted. But just like many other aspects of Socrates's thinking, his excessive pride in his likeness to Silenus escapes the understanding of the foolish. Flourishing hair is appropriate for little boys who are at the stage of life when we don't yet truly think, but in old age, which, as is clear, imparts intelligence and reason to a living being, it goes away and no longer remains. What else could you say except that this proves that the nature of hair is irrational? If someone has hair and is old, well, it's true some old men are foolish, and of course not all men develop into complete human beings. It thus stands that intelligence and hair can't tolerate one another, but like darkness and light, one gives way to the other. For those who want to know why, the answer is only for those initiated into the mysteries. Yet by limiting myself at present to only what's necessary, I'll try to keep everything sacred hidden under a veil of holiness.

7. Primary beings have a single form, but nature, as it descends, becomes varied. Matter is the lowest form of being and is thus the most varied. Even if it receives something of the divine, it doesn't at first receive it fully. Rather, matter receives impressions and "seeds" of the divine, which it enfolds and for the most part overwhelms, either by combining with what it has enfolded or by overpowering the divine element in the inevitable opposition at their initial encounter, before the impression reaches a state of completion. Either of these two ways is possible since these hypotheses aren't contradictory, as some think. But these matters aren't our concern at present—our interest lies elsewhere, and we only need to show on the basis of experience that nature holds sway over things that are in a state of incompletion, but yields to things that have reached their potential. And so even in the case of seeds that have been cast upon the earth, aren't their rational principles something divine, even if it's the lowest form of the divine? The final state of seeds is fruit, but observe the beautiful pageant of nature's development before they reach this state: roots, then stalk, then rinds, awns, and husks, and upon these husks yet other husks—but the fruit is still incomplete and not yet visible. But when the fruit comes into being, all these trifling bits of matter dry up and drop away, because what has reached its final state needs nothing

more to beautify it. The fruit is now complete since within it is another rational principle, a seed. (This is the reason for the mysterious "unveiling" of Demeter carried out at Eleusis.)[33] Now if intelligence is the most divine of the seeds that have descended from above and it resides in the head, and if embodied intelligence is its fruit (in the same way that wheat is the fruit of its rational principle), then nature is acting as it normally does. It works wonders on the head, glorifying it with beautiful hairs like the awns or husks or even, by Zeus, the flower that graces a plant before its fruit appears. But there's no fruit on a tree before the blossom falls, and intelligence can't exist in a head before it reaches perfection, with everything superfluous eventually scattered to the wind as if with a winnowing fan and all of nature's frippery stripped away. This state, then, can be taken as proof that the head has at last developed into a perfectly ripened fruit. And whenever you see a head clearly left bare, know that intelligence has taken up residence there and consider that head a god's temple. Mystery rites can be performed, called "Revelations of the Head" for the uninitiated, though the wise would know these are to celebrate the advent of intelligence. Who's initiated into these rites, who's admitted into the presence of the god? The man who's newly arrived at baldness. Wheat, pomegranates, and nuts can go bad and rot in their husk or shell, and so too heads go bad when they possess nothing of the divine and are mostly covered by dead matter. I myself have seen that priests in Egypt, servants of the divine, aren't allowed even to have eyebrows. They look ridiculous, but, being exceptional men and also Egyptian, they possess a certain wisdom, namely that natures that are eternal and whose essence is life shouldn't come into contact with elements that are dead. And if someone who becomes bald by his own hand is holy, then someone bald by nature has a natural bond with the divine. For isn't the divine itself also bald by nature? Then let it be favorable to my speech, for it will, of course, be delivered with pious intent!

8. So why would anyone trouble himself over any part of the divine that isn't visible, especially since it doesn't wish to show itself, not even once? And any visible part of it is a perfect sphere: the sun, the moon, and every star, both fixed and wandering,[34] all have this same shape, no matter their size. Could anything be balder than a sphere? Could anything be more divine? There's also the argument that the soul wants to imitate god. This is the third god, the soul of the cosmos, and its father, the demiurge of the corporeal cosmos, introduced it into the cosmos; from nothing but seeds and corporeal bodies he created the entire cosmos as something complete and perfect, and for this reason also shaped it into most comprehensive of forms. Given shapes whose perimeters are of equal length, the shape with more angles will always be greater in area. Among figures on a plane, a circle is greater than any polygon, and among figures with depth, a sphere.[35] Anyone with an understanding of geometry in two and three dimensions knows this. The soul in its totality animates the entire cosmos, which is a sphere. Souls flow out of this totality, becoming its individual parts, and each individual soul wants the same things as the soul in its totality: to govern bodies and be the soul of a cosmos, and this is the reason they're separated into individual parts. Consequently, nature developed a need for individual spheres. Thus the stars above as well as our heads below were fashioned to be homes for souls, microcosms within the cosmos, because the cosmos was to be a living thing composed of living things. For simpler souls, it's of no consequence if they inhabit a hairy head that falls far short of the perfect shape, but each wise soul receives an allotment according to its merits—one gets a star, another a bald head. For even if nature down here on earth lacks the capacity to be perfectly accurate, at least it doesn't allow the visible part of us that's highest and closer to the heavens to be anything but a cosmos in shape. A bald head has thus revealed itself to us as a heaven, and anything you could say in praise of spheres could also be said of bald heads.

9. Let Homer compose and Phidias sculpt, if he wants, representations that support Dio by draping Zeus with hair (and thick hair at that) with which he can move the heavens whenever he wants. The Zeus we see in the heavens[36]—we all know what he's like. But if there's also another Zeus, I'm not sure it's one that has a body. Suppose this other Zeus exists, if that's what someone wants to believe—he'd still have to be either the primary Zeus or the secondary one, in which case he's an image of the prior one. Either way, he's just like the Zeus visible to everyone, at least to the extent the working of nature allows the two to look the same. Yet poetry and sculpture (or any kind of representation for that matter) seem to have almost no concern for truth, but are concerned above all else with popularity. These arts do what they to win fame, not to find truth.

Hair is something the ignorant honor, and popular opinion marvels at everything superficial—property, chariots, houses, estates, and anything else that's not part of its possessor's nature, but rather, like hair, is disconnected from it. This is because the masses are far removed from intelligence and from god, and what's even more of a disconnect, nature and chance guide them instead of intelligence and god. As a result, the ignorant heap praise upon every gift of chance and nature. Anyone who writes for the people and speaks for the people must by necessity hold to popular opinions, and thus his compositions and orations are based on what pleases them. In fact, because the people are uneducated, they're "stiff-minded"[37] and stubborn guardians of their absurd beliefs, so if anyone does anything to unsettle what they're accustomed to, he soon drinks hemlock.[38] What do you think the Greeks would've done to Homer if he'd told the plain truth about Zeus without any of the outlandish tales that terrify little kids?

10. Another example of the wisdom of the Egyptians: in order to avoid committing any kind of sacrilege, members of the temple priesthood won't allow craftsmen or artisans to create images of the gods. Instead, curve-beaked falcons and ibises carved upon the outer walls of their temples dupe the people, while the priests themselves descend into their sacred pits and wrap up whatever's reached its final state.[39] For their final resting place they have small chests that, as they claim, conceal spheres—seeing them would anger the masses, and they'd most likely laugh in mockery (they need to have their fairy tales). How could they not, since it's the common people we're talking about? This is why ibis beaks are placed on all their statues. But one god they don't hide but display openly is Asclepius, and you can see he's balder than a pestle.[40] The Asclepius in Epidaurus has hair?[41] Well, the Greeks are "lethargic in the pursuit of truth," as a writer has justly criticized them.[42] Moreover, the Egyptians see Asclepius on a daily basis and pass time with him in conversation, and not only at his public altar nor only in the manner or time of his choosing. But I hear people say that an Egyptian man has techniques to deal with the gods, including certain spells, so that by babbling a bit in his strange language he can at will draw to himself any part of the divine that is naturally attracted by such powers. So truer images of the divine are to be found among the Egyptians, not the Greeks. And yet, as I said a little earlier, if you just look at the sun and stars there's no need to trouble yourself with a detailed inquiry. Even if there's a star with hair,[43] then it's no star, for the region of the stars is a body moving in a circle, and nothing new can ever happen there. But the region beneath the moon, the intermediate zone of generation, contains the combustible material wrongly called stars. In the former region, the stars move together in an orderly arrangement, while in the latter, they don't move in harmony since they don't share in the same nature. One of these "stars" made its way from the constellation Ara to the equinoctial sign, and from there it will travel until it reaches the North Pole, unless it perishes first. Some of these, as you'll notice, are of an immense length, and if today there should be one that extends over the entire length of the Zodiac, by the day after tomorrow it won't even be a third of its original length. It will continue on until the tenth or even thirtieth day, when after being extinguished little by little it vanishes, leaving behind not a single trace. I don't think it's at all pious to call these objects "stars," but if that's what you want to call them, wouldn't this mean hair is such a liability that even in the case of a star it produces a mortal form? It's a bad omen when these hairy stars appear, and soothsayers and seers try to appease them with sacrifices. Indeed, they presage disasters affecting entire peoples, like the enslavement of nations, the overthrow of cities, the deaths of kings—nothing minor or moderate, but terrible beyond measure:

> *no star from Zeus has perished into oblivion*
> *since the time our traditions began*[44]

Anything that perishes isn't a star; on the contrary, everything spherical is a divine body. I pray that I as well as all my relations receive this blessing[45] that makes me like the gods, because there are no others equal to the gods except those in this condition, no others for whom "godlike" or "godly" or any other term for divine beauty would be more fitting. And this is not one of those things where it ought to be the case but in reality turns out otherwise. In fact, you can hear people calling bald people to their face by the nickname "Moonie."

11. I nearly forgot to mention something that's quite relevant to my argument—the moon and its phases, whose names and shapes the bald share. My beloved moon begins as a crescent, becomes a semicircle, is then gibbous, and finally it's full. In fact, those who reach the summit of good fortune I call "full moons," though at this point it would be more appropriate to call them "suns." For no longer do they cycle through the phases, but with their perfect circle continually reflect the heavenly bodies, just like Odysseus when he was mocked by the suitors, more than a hundred of them, those young men with flowing locks soon to be utterly destroyed at the hands of one bald man. When he's getting a torch ready to provide some artificial light, they tell him to stop what he's doing since his bald head is sufficient to illuminate the entire house.[46] Isn't this the most divine thing of all, something the gods don't need to learn since it's part of their very nature—to possess and create light? A smooth surface creates a shine, and a smooth surface on the head occurs only in the complete absence of hair.

When someone moves away from what's worse, he simultaneously moves towards what's better (as when I said above that a corpse stands in opposition to a living body). Light and life and all such things are, and are thought to be, in the category of the good. If light is associated with baldness, then hair must be regarded as belonging with darkness. This isn't a probability—it's an unavoidable conclusion. Perhaps a dose of persuasion should be added to my argument, so as not to rely solely upon the force of rational demonstration. Well then, doesn't everyone think and say that those with hair are naturally shady? Archilochus, the most beautiful of poets, praised hair, and in particular praised a courtesan's hair as follows:

> *her hair casts a shadow over her shoulders and back*[47]

Shadow is no different from darkness, since both words signify an absence of light. By taking a closer look into the matter, anyone can see that the greatest shadow is night, since it's the earth blocking the rays of the sun. Even during the day densely wooded groves are deprived of light because they're overshadowed with excessively "hairy" foliage.

12. That's enough about the divinity of baldness and its connection to the brightest of the gods on high. If health is a good, and indeed the best of goods, I see that it's for this reason that many men with hair turn to the razor and depilatory creams in order to become simultaneously both bald and free of disease. If eye-sores, runny noses, earaches, and other such diseases of the head can be eliminated along with the burden of hair, this alone would be a great thing, but what's even greater is that it also benefits the feet and digestive system. Those with ailments in these areas are forced by doctors to endure a treatment called "cycles"—a depilatory cream is applied at the beginning, middle, and end of these cycles, and in attacking hair it's more relentless than a razor. And it makes sense that the "cables" of disease and health for the entire body run down from the upper part (that is, the head), as in the case of an acropolis. Therefore, we bald men don't have just an equal share of health, but, if god permits me to say so, an even greater one. It would seem that this also explains the hidden meaning of the wooden images of Asclepius made in the Egyptian manner.[48] These should serve as a public announcement, the healthiest prescription in all of medicine, and they all but exclaim, "if you want to be healthy, be like the inventor and patron of medicine!"

It wouldn't be surprising if a skull that basked in the sun and was exposed to every kind of weather soon turned from bone to iron. If this happened, it would be almost impossible for any disease to attack it. It's just like the way trees from the forest or the plains make worse spear-handles than trees from the mountains. For the reason why, ask Homer, and you'll hear him reply that the latter are *nurtured and trained by the wind*.[49] And don't think wise Chiron cut down a tree for Peleus' spear without putting some thought into it—he cut down a tree not from the nearby plain of Tempe, and not from a hill or ravine, where trees grow smooth and tall, but from the summit of Mt. Pelion, where they're exposed to blasts of wind.[50] That's why this wooden spear was good enough to be handed down to his descendants. It's the same with the two types of head, the hairy and the bald. One is of the meadow, since it's raised in shade, while the other is of the mountain, subjected to constant winds. As a result, the first is tender, the second, tough.

13. It's possible to find proof of this by visiting the spot where the armies of Cambyses and Psammeticus clashed, along the invasion route from Arabia into Egypt.[51] The two forces confronted one another in battle, and since each side believed this was the moment when all would be decided, only with great difficulty were they finally separated. After so much bloodshed and losses so heavy that the bodies couldn't be recovered, there was only one thing the survivors could do for the dead: since the corpses were mixed together in an indiscriminate heap, with each man falling where he was in the line of battle, they separated them into two piles of bones, one of Egyptians and the other of Medes. Herodotus was surprised to find that some of the skulls were very thin and fragile (it seems that this great man handled the skulls in a disrespectful manner): you could throw a pebble right through them, he says.[52] Others, however, were thick and sturdy. Hard and resistant to blows, not even a full-sized stone was sufficient to break through them—for that it would take a club. According to Herodotus, the explanation for this (and the reason why I've called upon his testimony as evidence) is that Medes wear felt caps, while Egyptians are raised with heads exposed to the sun. Even if it's too difficult to undertake a journey abroad to visit all the many different peoples, and even if it's sacrilegious to strike the head of a corpse (even if only with a stone), and even if you don't trust Herodotus, aren't there here in town servants both in my household and in many others who are Scythian and let their hair grow long in the Scythian fashion? You could rap their skulls with a knuckle and they would die.

At the theater there's a man who often puts on a good show for the people, and every month on festival days anyone who grabs a seat can catch his performance. He isn't naturally bald but made himself so by frequenting the barber day after day. His public appearances are a demonstration of his skull's strength. Nothing that's harmful can harm his head: he dunks it into boiling tar, butts heads with a ram trained to shake its head fiercely when launching an attack, and Megarian vases are left shattered against his noble skull. His head is covered in cuts and lacerations, and nothing done to it fails to send a shudder through the audience—it's pierced by needles more times than a finely embroidered Attic slipper. I myself saw this man, and when I did, I counted my blessings—I could've done all the same things! He, however, has more daring than me, or rather, poverty had led him to become so daring, while I have no need to try—and may I never have the need!

But there's a tremendous benefit that's different from this one, and it in no way falls short of the others mentioned.[53] If it's possible to fulfill the prayer of Pindar[54] and live on what we have, we'll pick out a good seat in the theater to see and hear whatever's put on for us. And if we need to be benefactors to the city and the people ask for charity, with a magnanimous spirit we'll be generous with what we possess. But if a demonic spirit opposes us and our daily bread runs short (may this never happen to any of the god-like men!), at least the worst of evils, starvation, won't be a problem for us, since we can all become wonderworkers and with only slight embarrassment appear on stage with an improvised display of skill worth seeing.

14. If anyone believes with Dio that hair is an attribute far more becoming to men than to women, doesn't he hold a position completely opposite to what is in fact the case, and obviously so? How does it make sense to grant to the strong possession of something that makes its possessor weaker? Of course, there's a distinction to be made between what's natural and what's conventional. If hair isn't something good for all males in all places at all times, then it's something conventional. And in fact, the Spartans wore their hair long after the battle of Thyrea, while the Argives did so before it,[55] and for many peoples this isn't a common practice, neither at present nor in earlier times. Yet for all women at all times and in all places, it's proper to be concerned with hair-care. There is not now nor has there ever been any woman who took a razor to her scalp, unless on account of some ill-omened or foreboding event—if in fact anything so terrible has ever happened (I've certainly never seen nor heard of it). And in this case, nature's in agreement with custom, since of all the women who've ever been born, not a single one has been revealed to be bald. And don't say they hide baldness under hair-nets, since comedies see right through these tricks.[56] If a woman has ever lost her hair, it was because of some disease, and with the slightest bit of care she could return to her natural state. As for men, at least those who deserve to be called such, it isn't easy to name one who hasn't arrived at this natural state, and for this very reason, baldness seems to be the perfection of nature, even if it doesn't happen to everyone. From observing the first shoots of healthy plants, farmers know that a plant naturally wants to grow straight up. However, many plants aren't strong enough to do this on their own, so they're supported with poles and stakes. In the same way, while all those whose nature is best appear in a state very much like my own, anyone who looks different needs a razor to give nature a helping hand and set him straight.

15. It's worth recalling the Spartans who tended to their hair before the battle of Thermopylae. Dio says this battle was great because the Spartans combed their hair before it, even though following this bad omen not a single one of them survived. I mention this not to repeat what I said earlier—that hair is something dead even when attached to something living—, but because the hairs of the dead continue to grow. At least this is what everyone has heard thanks to the priests in Egypt, and there was someone who died with a clean-shaven scalp but a year later had hair and a full beard. So Dio drags into his argument these men who of all the Greeks died the most noble death, but intentionally neglects to mention those who won the greatest and most glorious victories and took revenge on the barbarians on behalf of the Spartans and all of Greece: the Macedonians and Greeks who marched with Alexander, among whom only the Spartans were absent. Prior to the battle of Arbela (a battle with a better claim to be called great),[57] these men had learned from experience that long hair puts a soldier at a disadvantage, so they all cut their hair and with god, fortune, and courage on their side, they joined in a battle on behalf of all Greeks. Their aversion to hair had its origin in the following incident, as recorded by Ptolemy son of Lagos;[58] he knows about it since he was there when it happened, and because he was a king, he never lied when he wrote.

16. A Macedonian with extremely long hair and sporting a full beard attacked a Persian. Even though he was in danger, the Persian kept his wits, and he dropped from his hands the oblong shield Persians are known for and his spear, since these would be of no use against a Macedonian. Rushing at his enemy, he managed to evade his weapons and grabbed hold of his beard and hair. Throwing the defenseless Macedonian soldier to the ground, he yanked him up by the hair, like a fish, then drew his sword and killed the Macedonian while he was still on the ground. Another Persian saw this, and then another took notice, and then yet another. Soon they all dropped their shields, and with every man now grabbing his opponent by the hair, they drove the Macedonians from the field. Like an order for battle, word spread throughout the Persian army that these men could be taken by the hair. As you might expect, the only part of Alexander's phalanx still standing was bald. The king was now at a loss—invincible against the enemy when they were armed, he was beaten back by them when they were bare-handed! Alexander could have disgracefully retreated to Cilicia and become an object of ridicule to the Greeks, overcome in a battle of hair. Instead—since it was already fated that the Achaemenids would have to hand over their scepter to the Heraclids[59]—he soon realized what the danger was and ordered the trumpets to sound the retreat. Leading his men away as far as possible, he set up camp in a favorable spot and sent barbers there. Once the king presented them with gifts, they gave a haircut and a shave to every Macedonian. For Darius and the Persians, things no longer went as they hoped. Without anything to grab on to, they had to contend under arms with much better—and more handsome—opponents.

17. Thus, hair doesn't make men fearsome or even make them appear so, unless they're the bogeymen that scare children. And as we see in the case of soldiers, they put on helmets when they need to strike fear in the enemy. In both name and in reality, a helmet [*kranos*] is both nothing but a skull [*kranion*] made of bronze. As for helmets outfitted with horsehair crests, anyone who's had the opportunity to wear one understands their design. But anyone unfamiliar with them should realize that they're outfitted at the back with the hairs arranged in rows between the felt lining and the helmet itself. Not even Hephaistos could craft a helmet's convex surface to hold the hair in place, since given its shape, it offers a perfect image of baldness and is the most fearsome thing a soldier wears. Achilles says that the Trojans regained their courage not because they didn't see the horse-hair crests waving, but—how does it go?

> *they do not see the front of my helmet*
> *gleaming close by*[60]

The helmet's gleam and smooth surface would equate to baldness, and it would create fear. If Achilles had hair (he says he did, in fact)—well, he was young, at the age when he was still quick to anger and hadn't attained perfection in soul or body. It's quite likely, I think, that a young man's head would overflow with hair and his heart with emotion. But emotion in the soul isn't something that deserves praise because of Achilles, and neither is hair on the body something admirable. Of course, I'll admit that as the offspring of Thetis he possessed the greatest natural propensity for every virtue, and I'm of the opinion that if Achilles had lived, he wouldn't have been deprived of baldness or philosophy. Even in his youth he'd somehow learned some medicine and music, and as for the hair he had, he was so annoyed with it that after purifying himself, he cut off a lock of it as an offering to a sacred tomb.[61] Aristoxenes describes Socrates in similar terms, saying that he was "rough tempered"[62] by nature and, whenever he was overcome by emotion, he engaged in every kind of disgraceful behavior. Yet by no means was Socrates bald at the time, since according to Plato he was 25 years old when Parmenides and Zeno came to Athens to celebrate the Panathenaea.[63] But if someone had described Socrates as ornery or as having hair at a later age, I think this person would've become an object of complete ridicule to those who know anything, because Socrates was the baldest as well as the gentlest of all who have ever practiced philosophy. So don't condemn the hero Achilles for his hair, since when he spoke about it, he was a young boy just past puberty. And no one could say what evidence Dio relied upon when he declared that Achilles would've kept his hair even into old age. He wouldn't, in fact, have kept it, and I have plenty of proof: his father, his grandfather (I've seen portraits!), and his descent from the gods. And what I already said about the appearance of gods should be sufficient.

18. Why then do you cling to the following like a lucky charm you've stumbled upon?

she took hold of Peleus' son by his blond hair[64]

In short, why do you show us a snippet without putting the entire line on display? Well, since you won't, you leave us no choice but to do it:

standing behind, she took hold of Peleus' son by his blond hair

Well done, Dio! You removed some syllables that weren't at all superfluous, but in fact contained something completely contrary to what you intended. From this I surmise that even at this young age Achilles was going bald. The goddess came and grabbed his hair from *behind*, it says. Someone could grab me or Socrates or the oldest Greek there is from behind, since that's where the remaining signs of our mortal nature are. To be completely separated from association with everything mortal isn't a good that either a human or demon can possess, but clearly belongs to a destiny and nature that's divine.

standing behind, she took hold of Peleus' son by his blond hair

To grab his hair, she stood behind him, because in the front there wasn't anything to grab.

19. In general, there's nothing good about the nature of hair in Dio's speech. Yet if there were some good in it, Dio would've found it, and if it turned out to be something minor, Dio would have presented it as if it were the greatest thing. Even so, he managed to dig up Spartans from long ago who have nothing to do with his subject, at least not in the opinion of anybody but him. Tying himself to Homer like some sacred anchor, he keeps hold of him until the end of his text, but presents his argument in a totally illegitimate and purely rhetorical manner. In the present instance, he strikes something out of the line like it was some piece of legislation, while in others he cites as evidence parts of lines that don't actually exist. For example, he fabricates an obvious falsehood about Hector, or rather about what Homer says about Hector (or perhaps about both Homer and Hector at the same time). According to the way he's traditionally portrayed, Hector resembles the wisest of men in regard to his hairstyle, as was proven by someone who wrote about heroes with complete honesty (I believe he fought alongside some of them and fought against others, and he gives this same description of Hector).[65] If you visit Troy, as soon as you arrive some inhabitant will lead you to the shrine of Hector, where you can see a statue of him. Everyone who sees it is led to say that it portrays the way Hector looked when he scolded his brother for wasting time on his good looks, or in other words, for the careful attention he paid to his hair.[66] But this is what Dio put down as Homer's supposed description of Hector:

> *his dark locks were tossed about*

Let someone point out where in Homer's poem this is.[67] I'm certain not even Ion the rhapsode could find it![68] Could Homer have introduced into his poem a long-haired man who's then portrayed heaping abuse on some other man for his foppish behavior? It would be like Phileas accusing Andocides of temple-robbery when he himself was the one who pilfered Athena's Gorgon shield from the Acropolis![69] It's the same with your case against this hero.

20. If Menelaus had a *head of blond hair*,[70] in no way does this mean he had long hair, at least as can be gathered from the narrative. Nor is this mention of hair a compliment—it's only Homer informing us how things are, and just because Homer mentions something, it doesn't mean it's of a nature that makes it praiseworthy. It's clear that in order to supply himself with more examples, Dio treats any mention of hair as praise of it. How manly it was of him to add to the poem things that weren't there and to remove from it things that were in order to make a persuasive case that hair is far more becoming to men than to women! Even in the case of divinities, he says, Homer praises females in other ways, as with *ox-eyed Hera* and *silver-footed Thetis*, but Zeus he praises for his hair in particular. But maybe Dio's copy of Homer had quite a few good verses struck out of it, such as the following:

> *Lord Apollo, whom well-tressed Leto bore*[71]

and

> *placing him upon the knees of well-tressed Athena*[72]

When Hera schemes to make Zeus fall asleep, Homer says the goddess beautified herself in various ways, but needed the magical sash as well, since among its many different powers the greatest was stealing the wits from those who have them.[73] And in the same passage he says she put on perfume and:

> *combing her hair with her own hands, she pleated gleaming braids, beautiful and ambrosial*[74]

This one passage is deserving of a great deal of praise—deserving, indeed, even though it's an ambush against Zeus, given the numerous passages that one might say Dio neglected to mention. But in truth he knew them well enough, though he pretended not to. I know them, too, and I don't make up fake ones to prove my point, nor could I concede that any of the heaven-dwellers have hair. Whether they're male or female, my argument's the same: the Aphrodite among the stars appears in a form that's no less spherical than Zeus.[75] And as for Zeus, whom Dio used to crown his argument, what was said of him was in the same vein as Homer's other stories about the gods—most of it was said with a view to popularity, not truth. One of the things he said for the sake of popularity was the bit about the powerful hairs that hang from Zeus' head and shake the heavens, an idea both the masses and the statue-makers accept.

So if you eliminate Homer and the Spartans, there's nothing left to Dio's speech. But even if you include them, he tells us nothing about the nature of hair (as I said), neither finding anything of his own to say nor getting anything from Homer or the Spartans. He doesn't tell us what hair is, doesn't inform us of its qualities, doesn't demonstrate that it benefits those who have it or harms those without it. But this treatise of mine, after examining the very essence of the matter, found that baldness is something divine, is naturally related to divinity, and is the perfection of nature—a truly divine sanctuary where we acquire wisdom. It recounted the nature and the cause of countless other benefits for the body and the soul, such that nothing whatsoever has been asserted without clear reason. It's been shown that everything opposite to these goods is a characteristic of hair: lack of reason, brutishness, and anything which belongs to the class of things contrary to the divine. It's also been shown that hairs are just the husks and rinds of a living being, nature's frippery, the excrescence of an incomplete nature.

21. I think we ought to distinguish by type and by lifestyle the men extolled in my speech and those in Dio's. Aren't adulterers among those that love hair? In fact, Homer depicted a *virgin debaucher* with *curly locks* since he primped his hair for seduction, and the recipient of this reproach is in fact an adulterer, the best of them all.[76] This one type is the most treacherous and most like an enemy when within the walls of his fellow citizens. The people for whom we risk our lives in battle to prevent them from being raped (that is, our daughters and wives) are the very ones a gussied-up young man, if the opportunity presents itself, carries off to any place on land or sea he wants (and if not to some place on land or sea, then to some dark corner). And though it would be possible for the thoughts of a woman taken captive in war to remain true to the man she married, the very definition of an adulterer is a man who above all else steals from a woman's soul the warm feelings she has for the man she married. For the husband, the physical loss of his poor little wife isn't even the half of it. Understandably, then, the law puts weapons in the executioner's hands to use against them, and gardeners grow Attic radishes to deliver punishment as soon as one of them is caught.[77] This one type of man has brought many households to ruin, and in the past even some cities. In fact, adultery provided the pretext for conflict between two continents when the Greeks sailed to Priam's kingdom.

There's another type, much worse than the one for which Paris is the prime example, represented by men like Cleisthenes and Timarchus and all the rest who put their youthful beauty up for sale.[78] When this wasn't done for money, it was done in return for something else, and if wasn't in return for anything at all, then it was simply for the vile pleasure of it. There's no doubt that these men are all effeminate devotees of hair-care, and they're the ones who openly spend time at brothels (they think them the best, in fact, since that's where they can perfectly play the role of the female sex). But anyone who's perverse in private, but in public denies it, even if he shows no other sign of devotion to Cotys except carefully perfuming his hair and arranging it in curls, it would be immediately obvious to everyone that he celebrates the rites of the Chian goddess and her Ithyphallics.[79] Covering himself under his cloak, Pherecydes said

"The skin says it all," then showed his finger to make his illness known.[80] Likewise, a young man with unnatural desires can be known by his hair.

22. And if a proverb is wise—and how could proverbs not be, since Aristotle says they're fragments of the ancient philosophy lost during the great cataclysms that happen to mankind, and were preserved on account of their brevity and wit?[81]—the following verse is indeed a proverb, a saying whose value derives from the antiquity of the philosophy from which it originated, and we ought to take our time examining it, since the ancients had a much better eye for the truth than people today. So what is the proverb and what does it mean?

there's no one with hair who doesn't...[82]

You can add on the line-ending yourself by following the meter, since I don't dare utter it, frightful in name and in deed. Well done, you completed the line! So what do you think? Yes, indeed, it's the truth! It's an oracle, that's for sure. And its meaning is self-evident. And think how many witnesses it can call upon, both those who make use of it today and all those who used it in the past. What makes a proverb immortal is the long chain of people who utter it when some incident calls it to mind. Indeed, every time people see something happen, proverbs bear witness to it and supply precedents as proof.

23. But even though this is how things stand, Dio produced a marvelous speech on hair's behalf. Is there still a need of Plato to refute him when this rhetorician has made it abundantly clear that his rhetoric is just frilly hair-dressing? Or do you really think hair-dyers could make hair look more alluring after a man who speaks Greek has sung the praises of such a possession in the theater? I think those followers of Cybele[83] who've surrendered their manhood are extremely grateful to him for his speech, and so is anyone who gives his neighbor's wife illicit looks, since Dio doused each and every one of their heads with his words like they were perfume. Now to aim for something the public will admire is unavoidable, especially in the case of a man composing laudatory speeches after he's already won some popularity. And such a man is someone who would increase the population of utterly depraved men in our city.

But when it comes to baldness, what kinds of men does it set in opposition to these? What men have I praised instead of adulterers? Among them are priests, prophets, and acolytes found in the temples of the gods; teachers and instructors from the schools; generals and commanders in the military ranks (at least when things are going well); and from every walk of life men honored by the people for having more intelligence. And in my opinion, the singer whom Agamemnon left as a guardian for Clytemnestra was also of a type like me, since Agamemnon never would've entrusted a woman from a disreputable family to someone with hair.[84] Painters provide evidence for my argument when they're not painting from life, but instead someone claims to have found for them a model that corresponds to a way of life. For example, if an artist receives a commission to paint a picture of an adulterer or some sissy, he'll fulfill the commission if he takes a long-haired man as a model. If you should ask for a philosopher or priest, there'll be a painting of a rather grave-looking bald man, because baldness has been established by custom as their distinguishing feature.

24. To philosophers, priests, and all types who possess self-control, I offer this speech, presented with reverence towards the divine and good intentions towards men. And if, when presented to the public, it will be well received by the masses, so that lovers of hair, filled with shame, at last adopt a moderate and sensible haircut and deem happy those fortunate enough not to need a haircut, the thanks mustn't go to me for this. Rather, let thanks be to the subject of my speech, for it allowed the worst speaker to stand alongside the best. If I don't persuade anyone with my words, someone might fault my speech since even with the facts on my side I couldn't match the smooth charm of Dio's. But for the benefit of the masses, may this speech of mine, too, find its way into their hands!

Notes

1. Dio Chrysostom (ca. 40-115 AD), whose name means "golden mouth," was a famous orator and intellectual from Bithynia, a province in the north of modern-day Turkey on the shores of the Black Sea. Eight of his orations survive; the work in praise of hair is known only from the quotations by Synesius.

2. The Spartans invaded Attica at the beginning of the Peloponnesian War in 431 BC, cutting down and burning the olive groves surrounding Athens. See Thucydides, *The Peloponnesian War* 2.19-22.

3. *Iliad* 2.542. Synesius suggests that he was bald on top with hair in the back.

4. The third-century BC philosopher Epicurus believed gods existed, but only as confluences of very fine atoms unconcerned with humans or their affairs. For this reason, Epicureans were often accused of atheism.

5. "Aphrodite's business" is a euphemism for sex. Bellerophon, best known in mythology for killing the Chimera and capturing Pegasus, refused the advances of a king's wife who then falsely accused him rape; see *Iliad* 6.155-205.

6. Parysatis and her husband, the Persian king Darius II, had two sons. The elder, Artaxerxes, became king, but Parysatis supported the bid of the younger Cyrus to overthrow his brother. See Xenophon, *Anabasis* 1.1.4.

7. The "advocate" is Homer, whom Dio (and thus Synesius) quotes extensively.

8. Molione was the mother of Eurytus and Cteatus, said to be fathered by Poseidon. According to some sources, the sons shared a single body with two heads, four arms, and four feet. Augeas (owner of the stables that were one of Heracles' labors) made them leaders of his army against Heracles, who fell sick during the campaign, and thus Eurytus and Cteatus defeated his army and forced Heracles to retreat. Heracles later ambushed them and killed them. For the proverb, see Plato, *Phaedo* 89c.

9. Iolaos was the nephew of Heracles. See Apollodorus, *Library of Greek Mythology* 2.5.2.

10. Possibly a reference to the custom of dinner guests commenting in jest about each other's appearance. See Petronius, *Satyricon* 109.8, where a drunk Eumolpus wants to make fun of the bald.

11. At the beginning of book 20 of the *Odyssey*, the disguised Odysseus lies down to sleep while the the female servants who have been sleeping with the suitors are laughing and enjoying themselves. Odysseus briefly considers killing them but restrains himself. For the quotation, see *Odyssey* 20.23.

12. The Battle of Thermopylae in 480 BC, where under the king Leonidas the famous 300 Spartans defended to the death a narrow pass against the army of

the Persian king Xerxes. See Herodotus, *The Histories* 7.208, who describes the Spartans tending to their hair before the battle.

13. *Iliad* 2.477-79

14. *Iliad* 1.398; the epithet is used only of the Achaeans. Dio seems to take the epithet in a negative sense, or at least not as an attribute that could be considered beautiful.

15. *Iliad* 1.197

16. *Iliad* 3.284

17. *Iliad* 22.401-2. The Greek text quoted here by Synesius has a different verb than the Homeric texts.

18. *Iliad* 17.51

19. *Odyssey* 16.176. In Homer, this phrase refers to his beard, but either Dio or Synesius has substituted a different word.

20. *Odyssey* 14.230-31

21. *Iliad* 1.529

22. Plato, *Republic* 350d, where Socrates causes Thrasymachus to turn red after demolishing his claim that injustice is more advantageous than justice.

23. A phrase from the Greek comic playwright Alexis of Thurii (ca. 375-275 BC), whose works exist only in fragmentary quotations.

24. Both comb and stylus were made of reed.

25. Musical modes or tunings, associated with different styles of rhetoric.

26. See *Iliad* 1.189 (Achilles' "shaggy breast").

27. *Iliad* 23.151-53

28. Xenophon, *Cynegeticus* ("On Hunting") 4.1, says a dog's ears should be hairless on the back and the inside of the hips "smooth."

29. See Plato, *Phaedrus* 253e. Synesius uses a compound word λασιόκωφον ("hair-deaf"), found in a manuscript of Plato, for what should be two separate words ("hairy around the ears, and deaf").

30. Possibly a reference to the *mouseion* (museum, lit. "shrine of the Muses") connected to the library of Alexandria.

31. Likely Apollonius of Tyana, philosopher of the first century AD best known from the life of him written by Philostratus in the early third century AD.

32. Silenus is the leader of the satyrs who often accompanied Dionysus, particular in the orgiastic rituals. Satyrs, usually portrayed with an erect phallus, are

known for their lustful and lewd behavior stimulated by wine.

33. A reference to the Eleusinian Mysteries, one of the longest-lasting and most popular religious rituals of ancient Greece. Carried out in honor of Demeter, the Mysteries were held annually at Eleusis, on the coast of Greece not far from Athens, and lasted for several days. After rituals of purification and sacrifice, participants were shown sacred objects (the "revelation" or "unveiling"), the exact nature of which is unknown.

34. The "wandering stars" are planets, since they do not traverse the night sky in the "fixed" manner of the constellations. The word "planet" derives from the Greek word meaning "wander, go astray."

35. i.e., in three dimensions. According to this argument, a circle would consist of an infinite number of angles.

36. The planet Jupiter, named for the Roman equivalent of Zeus.

37. Aristotle says this is the name given to people who hold fast to their opinion (*Nicomachean Ethics* 1151b5).

38. A reference to the death sentence imposed upon Socrates.

39. Apparently a reference to hieroglyphics and mummification. A falcon represents the god Horus and an ibis *ba*, which in Egyptian belief was one of the elements corresponding to a person's soul. Both would be commonly seen on Egyptian tombs and temples.

40. Asclepius was a Greco-Roman god of healing. His shrines were prominent around the Mediterranean, and individuals with a particular ailment would make votive offerings in the form of the body part affected (numerous examples of small ears, eyes, legs, arms and other body parts exist). In same cases, the ill or injured individual would sleep at the temple, and Asclepius would visit them in a dream, sometimes in the form of a snake, to effect a cure (a procedure known as "incubation").

41. Epidaurus, on the Saronic Gulf in the eastern part of the Peloponnese (western modern-day Greece), was the site of the main shrine to Asclepius in the ancient world.

42. Thucydides, *The Peloponnesian War* 1.20.3

43. A comet, the Greek word for which means "haired," as in a "star with hair."

44. Aratus, *Phaenomena* 259-60 (an astrological poem of the third century BC).

45. i.e., baldness.

46. *Odyssey* 18.354-55

47. fr. 31 West

48. i.e., bald

49. *Iliad* 11.256

50. *Iliad* 16.143-44

51. Herodotus, *The Histories* 3.10-12

52. Herodotus, *The Histories* 3.12

53. i.e., a benefit to being bald. In this paragraph, Synesius is speaking on behalf of the bald, claiming no bald man has to worry about famine, since they could, if necessary, use their baldness to make a living like the theatrical performer just described.

54. Perhaps *Olympian* 5.23 ("if someone cultivates health and wealth").

55. Herodotus, *The Histories* 1.82

56. Synesius seems to refer to comic plays, though no specific example of this plot device is known (see Aristophanes, *Themophoriazousae* 138 for the closest example). One editor has suggested reading κωμμώτριαι (a rare word for a female servant) for κωμῳδίαι ("comedies").

57. The battle of Gaugamela in 331 BC, in which Alexander defeated the Persian king Darius.

58. A Macedonian general who following Alexander's death ruled as king of Egypt ca. 304-283 BC. Under his rule, Alexandria became a cultural capital of the Mediterranean world (the renowned library was established either by him or his son.) The dynasty he founded lasted almost 300 years, ending with the suicide of his famous descendant Cleopatra VII.

59. The Achaemenids ("descendants of Achaemenes") refers to the dynasty that ruled the Persian empire beginning with Cyrus the Great in 550 BC. Many Greeks, and the Spartans in particular, could claim to be descendants of Heracles ("Heraclids"), and rulers often visually associated themselves with Heracles by, e.g., being represented on coins and in statues with a lion-skin hood (from the labor of the Nemean lion) and a club, a weapon associated in particular with Heracles. In this case, "Heraclids" seems to refer to Greeks in general, but specifically the Macedonians under Alexander's command (whether the Macedonians were truly Greeks was a matter of dispute then as now).

60. *Iliad* 16.70

61. *Iliad* 23.141-53, at the tomb of Patroclus.

62. Plutarch, *Publicola* 3.1 (in reference to Brutus).

63. See Plato, *Parmenides* 127b-c.

64. *Iliad* 1.197

65. Philostratus of Athens' *On Heroes*, from the early third century AD, presents a dialogue between a "vinedresser" and a Phoenician traveler; the vinedresser claims to know the twice-resurrected Protesilaus, who died at Troy, and also sees other heroes of the Trojan War. The statue of Hector is described at 19.2, which specifically mentions his beauty μετ' οὐδεμιᾶς κόμης ("with no [long] hair"), and his disdain for long hair on account of Paris is mentioned at 37.3.

66. *Iliad* 3.55

67. The lines do in fact occur at *Iliad* 22.401-2, though with a different verb than in the quotation here (which has πεφόρηντο, "dragged, carried," instead of πίτναντο, "spread out."). It's possible Synesius' copy of the *Iliad* did not have these lines.

68. The eponymous interlocutor in Plato's *Ion* who boasts of his knowledge about the Homeric epics.

69. See Isocrates, *Against Callimachus* 57, where the name is Philourgos.

70. *Odyssey* 15.133

71. *Iliad* 1.36

72. *Iliad* 4.273

73. *Iliad* 14.215-17

74. *Iliad* 14.175-77

75. Referring to the astronomical objects we know as the planets Jupiter and Venus.

76. *Iliad* 11.385, where Diomedes mocks Paris.

77. It was a traditional punishment for adultery to shove a radish into the adulterer's anus. See Aristophanes, *Clouds* 1083.

78. Cleisthenes was an Athenian of the late fifth century BC, ridiculed numerous times by the comic playwright Aristophanes for his passive homosexuality, which Greeks considered unmanly (in contrast to being the active partner in a homosexual relationship). Timarchus is the target of a speech by the fourth century. BC orator Aeschines; one of the charges levelled against Timarchus is that he prostituted himself.

79. Little is known of Cotys, a goddess from Thrace associated with orgiastic rituals, for which reason she was later associated the Cybele. "Chian goddess" is obscure but may be Cotys. "Ithyphallic" means "with an erect phallus"; statues of various gods, including Hermes, Priapus, and Osiris, were sometimes ithyphallic, and the satyrs who attended Dionysus are also so represented.

80. Pherecydes was a Greek writer of the sixth century BC who combined cosmology and mythology. He was later regarded as something of a mystic, much like Pythagoras, about whom a similar anecdote was told (Diogenes Laertius, *Lives of the Philosophers* 1.118).

81. *Nicomachean Ethics* 1074b8

82. In Letter 104, Synesius quotes the line in full with the ending ψηνίζεται (a verb that refers to pollinating a fig tree but is used here in an obscene sense for sex).

83. Cybele, also known as as "Great Mother" (*Magna Mater* to the Romans), was a goddess whose male followers were infamous for dancing to cymbals and drums and in their ecstatic state castrating themselves.

84. *Iliad* 3.267-68

HUCBALD OF SAINT-AMAND
ON BALD MEN

[Introductory verses in praise of the bald]
Polymnia, muse honored by poets, slow your step:
in haste to behold bishop Hatto's[1] cheerful visage,
fulfill the solemn duty you display in your name.[2]
Compose monuments in remembrance of men of old,
men who, we know, did not displease the poets' Muses—   5
instead they lavished them with gifts, a poem's reward.
The world stands as witness to what his Muse brought Maro,
scion of Mincio's streams[3]—his sayings spread everywhere.
And what about Ovid, and what about Porphyry, poets
whose sentences of exile the Muses once commuted?[4]   10
There was once some Greekling who often paid Augustus
homage in verse, but as a reward received nothing.
He refused to fetter his presumptuous Muses
until he extracted two verses from the mighty prince;
then he paid him a couple of coins for his couplet,   15
hinting at his wealth. So he chided the greedy king,
and for this first outlay was repaid with interest![5]
Another example: there was a crow who could say
"Hail, Caesar!" His greetings unreturned, the crow complained
that his teacher's best efforts had all been for nothing—   20

Augustus then purchased the crow for a hefty sum.[6]
In days of yore, by custom of the high and mighty
this law held good when it came to musical poets:
they would not lament that they'd worn out their lips piping
without recompense, that their efforts were all for naught.   25
Alas! Should this law expire, so would all efforts
to educate, when no honor's bestowed upon art.
Alas! Could anyone who's found guilty of this charge
properly be called a true prince and potentate?
If the dactylic muses fall silent, who, I ask,   30
will compose poems of praise for bald beauties? Who, I ask,
will silence mouths barking in mockery at the bald?
Hurry up, close ranks, gleaming baldheads, please bring us aid!
And you, great and worthy baldy, pride of the chromedomes,[7]
answer our prayers, and with all good fortune, greetings!   35
Perusing with proper prudence this paltry present,
marvel at the Muses' modulated melodies!
Here, for you, one hundred, thrice ten, and twice three verses.
The letter that marks "hundred" starts the name for the bald,
adorns our faces with the form of a moon's crescent,   40
and shapes the stage[8]—it also encompasses our poem,
circling back to start each line and every word.
The croaking crow caws to you in greeting, my great prince!
But not to pour out pleas in return for a favor
nor to complain about efforts expended for naught—   45
let no one have any cause to say, think, or believe
that I, who crafted these verses in praise of the bald,
am robbed of my reward. I profit from the greatest
of gifts: to know one whom all admire in all ways,
to know this excellent bishop deems me worth knowing.   50
When the King of Kings sits in judgment over the world,
I pray that he will place him among the blessed popes,
and grant him fellowship in the heavenly kingdom.
"So may it be, amen!" resounds the all-bald chorus.

ON BALD MEN
A poem in 136 pangrammatic verses

Cantos were composed by a curly crank[9] criticizing
chromedomes? Celebrate, *per contra*, in a choice canto
conspicuous chromedomes! Comprehend, crowd, this canto.

[*Prooemium: The Muses are summoned to praise the bald*][10]
Chant, Clio's clear-voiced coterie, cantos for chromedomes!
Contriving to coif chromedomes in a condign canto,   5
conversely I'll confound curls on crested craniums.
Clever consorts of Clio, celebrate my clear canticles:
Commend chromedomes and castigate the curs
conspiring to carp at conspicuous cleanheads with crimped cackling.
Chromedomes' cause, command the cosmos!   10
Capillose crowd, with clotted curls, clam up—
cease chastising the chromedomed crowd with crazed cant!
Chant concordant cantos in conjunction with chromedomes!

[*I. That baldness seems to happen to some as a prophecy of the future*]
Chant, Clio's clear-voiced coterie, cantos for chromedomes!
Collar culminates in the crown of a chromedome?   15
Consider certain the chromedome's a cleric's consort,
capturing the conspicuous crown Christ confers.
Cutting like curls crimes from the cardium,
cardiacally he contemplates the Creator, the created cosmos carnally.
Chafing to commune in cultus with celestial citizens,   20
crimes commingled with cursory cares he condemns completely.
Comprehending the celestial cornice and cherubic concord,
concupiscently he commends the creator of the cosmos.

[*II. Bald men are cantors, abbots, and doctors, as well as bishops and priests*]

Chant, Clio's clear-voiced coterie, cantos for chromedomes!
Canorous chromedomes celebrate with conspicuous clamor,   25
chaste choruses continue the chorale.
Cerebrally conformed, corporeally concordant,
clerics compete to convene cordial congregations.
Clutching coronets, celestial cohorts clash,
completing the cherished chrism of Christ's call,   30
converting confused companies into chrismatized cohorts.
Confederated they carefully celebrate with comestibles,
companions consuming Christ's corpus and cruor.

[IIa. *Bald men are monks, psalmists, and grammarians, as well as poets and
scribes, possessed of the greatest self-control*]
[Chant, Clio's clear-voiced coterie, cantos for chromedomes!
Countless chromedomes congregate in chaste camps.   35
Contending to celebrate Christ in celestial choirs,
carnal curls cropped, they cogitate cosmic creation,
covet the celestial, curb cursory cares,
compile compositions, concoct conspicuous cantos,
carefully copy with certitude the Catholic canon,   40
consume chow, collect a constantly chaste cardiac calidity,
contend, like couriers circumnavigating
common courses, to climb the celestial cornice.][11]

[III. *Bald men are kings and emperors, as well as consuls, legislators, and judges*]
Chant, Clio's clear-voiced coterie, cantos for chromedomes!
Chromedomes, in control, command the celestial cornice,   45
conspicuously capped with a collucent crown.
Clement in collecting customs, they counsel cases for clients:
Careful, curly, chromedomes condemn crimes!
Chromedomed censors confirm the count:
Caution! A chromedome is clever, courageous,   50
considers a calumniator of chromedomes crippled in his corneas!
Cease to carp caliginously at a chromedome's clean crown,

cease corrosive comments about chromedomes—cease!

[IV. *Bald men are leaders of armies and are themselves warriors, intelligent and brave*]
Chant, Clio's clear-voiced coterie, cantos for chromedomes!
Chromedomes command conspicuous columns in conflict.   55
Chromedomes in combat, covered by crested caps,
cut down, chop-chop, counterposed chiliads,
capture curly-heads, crush the capillose,
chomp them with cuspids; with coruscant cuts, craniums
collapse. Clamoring chromedomes crow commands—   60
compelled to clash, a chromedome clever in conflict
crushes, conquers, coerces curly-heads to capitulate.
Capturing captives, he constrains the captured by the collar.

[V. *Praise of bald men in the field of medicine, pharmaceutics as well as surgery*]
Chant, Clio's clear-voiced coterie, cantos for chromedomes!
Confirm chromedomes contribute to the cerebral constitution,   65
confirm chromedomes cure cranial catarrhs,
confirm chromedomes correct corporeal cavities!
Chronic contagions and cancer capitulate to chromedomes,
cardiac-cramping contagions are checked, colic ceases.
Controlling cutters, he corrects with carnal carving   70
cranial cruor corrupted by a cankered collar-bone.
Can I continue the compliments? He counteracts completely
concealed causes of convulsions, cures corporeal calamities.

[VI. *Polemical attack against a caviler criticizing chromedomes*]
Chant, Clio's clear-voiced coterie, cantos for chromedomes!
Careful, curly, not to callous-heartedly contravene the Creator,   75
cease to cast calumny on his creation!
Commanding causes completely, the Creator constituted
creation, careful to confer care on creatures cowed into
consenting to a chromedome's clear cornice

cropping up, then compelled to complete capitulation.   80
Crazed cur, why cry with canine clamor
"Chromedomes were created from a calabash cast into clay"?
Cruddy calumny to be cursorily censored!

[VII. *More against the caviler, as well as praise of the humility, charity, and chastity of the bald*]
Chant, Clio's clear-voiced coterie, cantos for chromedomes!
Companion of criminals, why choose to carp at a chromedome's   85
carnal covering? Chromedomes carve away crimes of character.
Could you choose to cover a chromedome's crown with cinders?
Chromedomes comprehend the carnal corpus is created from cinders.
Could you conclude the carnal corpus is cremated with calid charcoal?
Chromedomes cremate cardia cooked with Christ's calidity.   90
Could you conclude a chaste chromedome is carnally castrated?
Castrated completely to the core of culpability.
Choral carver of chromedomes, curb your caviling!

[VIII. *Criticism of his poem and, as an example for the critic, the prophet Elijah and the boys who insulted him*]
Chant, Clio's clear-voiced coterie, cantos for chromedomes!
Conjoining cryptic chants to clear I caution against.   95
Contemptible calumny must be crushed under a crud-caked clog—
cork your cane-flute, cruddy chanter of crud!
Confirmed by the codex: a clear-sighted chromedome,
completely conscious of the celestial, is a careful critic.
Confounded by a circle of cacophonous children clamoring   100
"Clear out, chromedome!", the chromedome cursed those curs.
Consequently their crime of calumny was clear:
corpses clawed, chewed up in chunks, they croaked.[12]

[IX. *The famously bald apostle Paul, called by Christ, was blinded and taken up to third heaven*]
Chant, Clio's clear-voiced coterie, cantos for chromedomes!

Calvous chants cumulate with the chants of a conspicuous   105
cleanhead, whose cruel caution committed him to carving up
cultivators of Christ with cuts. Celebrate the confused chromedome's
coruscating charisma! Called by Christ's clamor,
curtly he collapsed, comparably to a conk from a cane's cusp.
Cursorily he completed the caerulean climb,   110
catching a clear conception of coexistence with the all-capable—
clearly his cardium came to be a celestial container.

[X. *A persecutor turns preacher, and he forbids the growing of hair and profane talk*[13]]
Chant, Clio's clear-voiced coterie, cantos for chromedomes!
Collect your choirs, chant in cadence about chromedomes.   115
Certainly we caught on, a cherished chromedome
changed his celebrated censure. The celestial chief cognizes
conspiracies of a conniving chanter of crimes, completely constrains
cruddy colloquies, considering the crowd's common comforts.
Confounding curly-heads, civic-mindedly he constitutes colleges.   120
Conciliatorily, he cues the concerns of Christian co-advocates,
contriving to conjoin congregation to its chief.
Cease, curly, carping at celebrated chromedomes!

[XI. *The poet addresses the Muses about a critic, insinuating that he was blinded by the judgement of the bald king*]
Chant, Clio's clear-voiced coterie, cantos for chromedomes!
Constrain the captive criminal cruelly contriving   125
criticism of all chromedomes—a cracked-up contention!
Confine in caliginous caverns one convicted in a cinch,
contriving crazed conspiracies of conflict.
Censorious chromedomes condemn one criminally charged,
corneas cloaked: cease, canine, carping carelessly at chromedomes!   130
Cower, canine, who contrives crimes against chromedomes!
Cower, canine, who clamorously chants at chromedomes!
Cower, canine, cease chomping at chromedomes!

[XII. *Summary of the praise of the bald based on physical beauty, and the bald man as microcosm*]
Chant, Clio's clear-voiced coterie, cantos for chromedomes!
Cognizing clearly that a company of cleanheads   135
comprises a coruscant collection, comprehend the cosmic circle is
chromedomed.
Consider a cleanhead's crown the center of the cosmos.
Characteristics of chromedomes compare to the cosmic circuit.
Connect with cleanheads, convene candescent chromedomes—
Cynthia[14] will cease comparisons to chrysanthous colors,   140
clouding her curves she cedes crescents to chromedomes.
Crystalline chromedomes, candescent caps of cleanheads,
coruscate crimson like the clear cosmic conglomerate.

[XIII. *Conclusion of the poem and praise of bald men*]
Chant, Clio's clear-voiced coterie, cantos for chromedomes!
Close up in cases cane-reeds celebrated for composing, correctly: 145
complete is the cadenced canto for celebrated chromedomes.

[*The following verses, addressed to the emperor Charles the Bald, were printed by von Winterfeld.*]
Careful, clarion Camena, of cheating chromedomes in chant!
Contrarily, cowardly calumny from crimped curls can collapse.
Chromedome charms chanted in clarion cadence
can clam up when, coaxed with canorous clanging,
celestial creation collapses in celebration of Christ.   5
Caesarean chalices and cautious Cato's clever coffer[15]
can contain chants criticizing clerical culpability.
Conclude, Camena, chromedome's companion, chanting!
Charles, celebrated Caesar, chant with chromedomes
contentions of a conspicuous cleric for Christ crucified.   10
Camena, congenial with Caesar, in conclusion cares.
Curl-covered crown, careful! Chants celebrating chromedomes,
contrived with a cleanhead Caesar, collect coins.
Christ, whose cross is clemency for chromedome crimes,
consider chromedomes conjoined with curly-heads!

Notes

1. Archbishop of Mainz (Moguntinus) from 891 until his death in 913.

2. The name of the muse, which should be broken down as *Poly-hymnia*, is here understood as *Poly-mnia*, "much remembering."

3. A river in northern Italy, tributary of the Po, which runs through Mantua, the birthplace of Vergil, here called by his *cognomen* Maro.

4. The poet Ovid (43 BC-17 AD) was exiled by the emperor Augustus to Pontus, a region by the Black Sea, in 8 AD. While there, in addition to the *Metamorphoses* he wrote the *Tristia* ("Sorrows") and *Epistulae ex Ponto* ("Letters from Pontus," sometimes called "Letters from Exile"). Publius Optatianus Porfyrius (ca. 265-335 AD) was a poet known for "pattern-poems" and a public official under the emperor Constantine, by whom he was exiled for reasons unknown. He wrote a collection of poems in praise of the emperor, from whom he begged forgiveness.

5. The anecdote is found in Macrobius, *Saturnalia* 2.4.31.

6. Macrobius, *Saturnalia* 2.4.30

7. Charles the Bald (Charles II), grandson of Charlemagne, king of West Francia and then Italy until he succeeded to the Carolingian throne in 875, but died only two years later. Scholars have debated whether his moniker "the bald" should be taken literally, since images of him represent him with hair. Literary sources, however, suggest he was in fact bald.

8. "C" is the sign for one hundred and the first letter of *calvus*, "bald." The theater is an amphitheater, shaped like a "c."

9. Denis proposed *cirritus* (curly-headed) for *cerritus* (crazy). Regardless of the reading, a pun is likely intended.

10. The section titles found in manuscripts are likely later additions.

11. This section, missing from some manuscripts, was likely not part of the original, since its inclusion would bring the total number of lines to 146 rather than the 136 specified in line 38 of the introductory verses.

12. 2 Kings 2:23. After the young boys mock Elijah, two she-bears come out of the woods and maul them.

13. 1 Corinthians 1:14; Ephesians 4:29

14. Epithet of the goddess Diana (Greek Artemis), here as the moon.

15. Perhaps a reference to the chests filled with money to which Cato attached cork-floats with long ropes so they could be found in case of shipwreck (Plutarch, *Cato the Younger* 38.1).

BURCHARD OF BELLEVAUX
A DEFENSE OF BEARDS
ADDRESSED TO THE LAY-BROTHERS

A defense by Burchard, abbot of Bellevaux, to the brothers of Rosières, for the preservation of their beards and for their salvation.

Since I'm going to deliver a shaggy-sounding sermon on beards, perhaps I'll be called a "barbilogist."[1] In fact, this sermon about your beards, brothers, is a defense, because you've accused me of declaring an anathema of burning against your beards.[2] Far be it that such a barbarous thought ever enter my mind—to desire your beards to be set aflame! Whoever wrongly inferred that the anathema against beards applied to yours spoke falsely against his own. In fact, just as our brothers' beards (or anyone else's) aren't excluded from the anathema of burning if they knowingly do anything mentioned in the letter,[3] your beards aren't included under any obligation to be set ablaze as long as you commit no wrong for which they would deservedly pass through fire and become fodder for the flames.[4] Therefore, if you're free of guilt, you shouldn't apply anything about beard-burning in that letter to your own beards. However, neither the beards of our brothers nor of any other brothers are exempt if they should fall into an error that merits the punishment of burning. I want your beards to remain untouched, far from the flames, so don't let them cause me harm! For your beards would indeed cause me harm if because of them you think that I've offended you and you banish me from the grace of your affection—me, who was like family to you before this matter of beards arose! If I did speak ill of beards and I wasn't allowed to say what I'm accused of saying, then may my beard cease to grow, or let there no longer be a need to shave it and I become like a woman—beardless! And what did I say about beards? "The beards of those who knowingly and intentionally stir up a storm that makes shipwrecks of men's souls should *be burned as fodder for the flames*!"[5] Who would dare criticize this view except someone who's ignorant, beardless, and (because he lacks a beard)[6] childish? Who wouldn't instead proclaim "So be it, so be it!", if indeed it's more righteous to burn beards than to imperil souls?

SERMON I
THE CLEANLINESS OF BEARDS

Chapter 1. *Beards should be kept clean of three types of vermin, following the example of Aaron*

To preserve your beards in a pristine state, I hope and desire you'll follow the example of Aaron's beard. That is, just as *the oil on the head that flowed down onto the beard, the beard of Aaron*[7] produced cleanliness and purity in his beard as an allegory for all beards, so too let the spiritual ointment of Jesus Christ flow down from your head onto your beard. It purges and purifies all your inner thoughts, where a man's vitality and the venerable maturity that comes with age manifest themselves, and it's appropriate that beards exhibit this quality. So if you have a sincere desire to bring your inner beards in line with your outer beards, you shouldn't ignore the proper treatment of your beard's outer appearance.

Chapter 2. *The three kinds of vermin and the ointment (that is, the virtues) that keeps them clean*

You know full well that beards should be kept clean and free of the three kinds of vermin.[8] If beards aren't carefully maintained in a state of cleanliness, then something wretched and truly awful happens: swarming out from the inner beard will appear lice, a disgusting mass of nits, and a third kind of vermin (said to take its name from "foot in eye").[9] However, a careful precaution against this happening in the outer beard is to ensure the inner beard is kept clean and pure. And how else could this happen if not by the oil *that flowed down onto the beard, the beard of Aaron*? These vermin cannot hatch in beards that have been anointed with this kind of oil, following the example of Aaron. This oil flows down onto the inner beard, where there's the *love that comes from a pure heart, a good conscience, and a sincere faith.*[10] Consider how this oil keeps beards clean and pure by using this three-fold division of virtue to destroy the three kinds of vermin: purity of heart removes the lice, integrity of conscience eliminates the swarms of nits, and sincerity of faith utterly destroys the third kind, named from "foot in eye."

Chapter 3. *The different characteristics of the three types of vermin and their connection to three vices*

Something else rather remarkable about beards and worth reflecting upon is that these three types of vermin are distinguished by their own particular traits. The first type clings to the skin and doesn't move into the hairs, the second holds fast to the hairs and stays there, while the third moves back and forth between skin and hairs. Blessed and pure are the beards of those who have no knowledge or experience of these! The three vices are sensuality, indecency, and duplicity. Note how sensuality clings to the flesh like lice and doesn't dwell among the hairs, because it doesn't want to show itself openly in anything associated with manly adornment, beauty, or virtue, but prefers to lurk in the shadows. Sensuality lives in the slothful, the sluggish, and the lazy; every lazy man lives in his desires and desires destroy the slothful man. This is the meaning of the lice that infest beards.

Indecency debases the external signs of dignity, and attacks, so to speak, the hairs of the beard when it marshals against the respect owed to a mature age all the various frivolities of its depraved excesses—this is the disgusting swarm of nits that gather on the beard. The interpretation suggested by the fact that this wretched corruption doesn't leave the hair and move onto the skin seems to be that those who pay heed *to vanities and illusory obsessions*[11] are outwardly fixated on their vain excesses and cling fast to their social reputation with an unyielding stubbornness. As a result, such people give the appearance of completely neglecting the care of the flesh. People who want to look wise behave this way in order to make others think they're philosophers, and they use their beards to make a show of their respect for wisdom. Yet, as is clear, these vile, disgraceful wretches nourish in their beards nothing but a multitude of nits.

Duplicity is the third vice in beards, and it takes its name from "foot in eye" because *a man duplicitous in spirit is inconstant in all his ways,*[12] just as this kind of vermin runs back and forth between the skin and the hairs. The first two kinds of vermin don't move, while the third does. Clearly visible in both the beard and the hair, it can also be easily recognized among the vices if looked for with attentive care. But why does this third type of vermin take its name from "foot in eye," such that it can be interpreted as the vice of duplicity and every beard can rightly be cleansed of it? Because the foot's function is to tread the ground while the eye signifies disposition and affection. "Foot in eye," that is, foot next to the eye, can only mean that the intention (or disposition and affection) is never raised up from earthly matters. If, on the other hand, someone has his feet on the ground and his eyes towards heaven, he can say: *My eyes are always towards the Lord.*[13] Let the feet and eyes remain far apart, and there will be neither "foot in eye" nor duplicity in the soul.

And so, brothers, in order to maintain the purity of your beards, you should never be without the oil of a pure heart, a good conscience, and an unfeigned faith.[14] Sensuality has no place in a pure heart, indecency doesn't come near a good conscience, nor duplicity near a true faith. Whoever doesn't realize this doesn't have a clean beard, since the oil doesn't flow onto his beard like the oil *that flowed down onto the beard, the beard of Aaron.*

Chapter 4. *The moral interpretation of why Aaron's beard is named with a doubled appellation*

Why is the beard of one man, which is only a single beard, doubled to say *onto the beard, beard*? It can only be because the allegorical meaning of this one beard applies to many beards. As many lay-brothers are bearded in imitation of a single bearded lay-brother, so the allegorical meaning of this single beard should be honored in its application to many beards. From this beard lay-brothers should understand why they must have beards, since there can be no doubt whom they ought to imitate by having beards. For your beards, dear brothers, are also cleansed by an application of oil, just like Aaron's beard was cleansed by the oil that flowed down onto it.

Chapter 5. *Leprosy in the beard, its allegorical cleansing, and the signs indicating the presence of leprosy in the beard*

This oil is needed not only for the disgraceful conditions mentioned above, but also for the leprosy that often afflicts beards. If you do not believe me, ask Moses, or rather the Lord who is in Moses. I'll excerpt from the relevant passage the part that concerns us, brothers. He said: *In whose beard leprosy has taken root, let a priest see him.*[15] If someone considers himself wise or boldly boasts of his righteousness, he has leprosy in his beard, because a beard signifies wisdom and strength as well as beauty and virtue. In recognition of this, a priest, whose duty is to care for souls, should try to cleanse the beard of leprosy. Moreover, whoever falls into heresy and blasphemy because of his learning has clearly contracted leprosy in his beard. Further evidence that there's leprosy on the head and in the beard is provided when he says: *And if the place is lower than the other flesh and there is blond hair, finer than normal, he* (that is, the priest) *will pronounce them unclean, because it is leprosy of the head and beard.*[16] That is to say, if the intention behind someone's thoughts abandons its proper place and he becomes more intelligent in finding evil, he shall be condemned. Leprosy in the hair is an error in thought, while leprosy in the beard is an intelligent intention for evil, according to the saying: *They are wise to do evil.*[17] On the other hand, there are signs that prove leprosy isn't present in the hair or beard, when he adds: *But if he sees a blemish level with the neighboring flesh and black hairs, he will quarantine them for seven days, and on the seventh day he will make an examination. If the blemish has not grown, and the hair keeps its color and the location of the disease is the same as the rest of the flesh, let the man be shaved around the area of the blemish and let him be kept inside for another seven days. If on the seventh day the disease has not spread and is not deeper than the rest of the flesh, he will pronounce him clean; his clothes will be washed and he will be cleansed.*[18] The entire sequence of this passage allegorically illustrates the character of a man's thoughts by means of the hair and of his intelligence by means of the beard. As a result, we can recognize, thanks to to the teaching of the seven-fold Spirit,[19] that when the error is small, there's little deviation from the true path and the hair and beard maintain their usual dignity, but if someone shamefully wanders far from the truth, his beard then becomes a mess and his hair falls out in condemnation of the head—this is what it means to have a foul leprosy in the hair and in the beard. But if this person should persist in his disgraceful behavior, all of it will be condemned to burning, as later verses declare.[20] However, if the judgment is for renewal by the cleansing of correction, his head and beard will be subjected to shaving and washing so that new hair and a new beard will grow. You too, bearded brother, if you glory in your advanced age or your life of piety, if you scorn your juniors and insult them, setting your years above their youth, *go and show yourself to the priest,*[21] for you have leprosy in your beard.

Chapter 6. *The "flying and wandering" leprosy of the beard and its moral interpretation*

But if the leprosy afflicting a beard is *flying and wandering,* as described in that passage, the beard is sentenced to destruction by fire.[22] That is, if you don't reform and, even though you've often confessed and been corrected, your disgrace constantly flies back to you and in its wandering doesn't remain in the grief of penitence, rest assured that the fires of hell await you and have been called down upon you. This is why in other writings I declared (but didn't desire!) that beards *be burned as fodder for the flames*[23]—it's on account of the leprosy in them. But if in this matter you believe and judge that I've contracted this error (or leprosy), then, my dear brothers, take my beard, shave it off, and burn the whole thing. For then I will be well, if the leprosy of my error shall perish along with my beard.

Chapter 7. *The beard of David, the saliva flowing over it, and its moral interpretation*

There's a disgrace beyond reckoning that happens to beards, and while it has a disgusting outward appearance, and is therefore something to be avoided, in its inner meaning it's something everyone with a beard should desire out of a love of virtue. Anyone whose beard is covered with saliva you despise and consider contemptible. Those of you who have a love of dignity and cleanliness exclaim, "We won't become so unkempt and dirty that we defile our beards with streams of spit!" Bearded David, step forward and respond to these bearded ones who in their confusion are ashamed to hear what you were not ashamed to do! You feigned insanity before king Achish, you altered your face to look like a man overcome by madness, and saliva ran down your beard. *And Achish said to his servants: Look at that madman, why did you bring him to me? Are we so lacking in madmen that you brought him here to rave before me? Will he enter my house?*[24] Brothers, are your beards purer and more glorious than the beard of the divine David, the glorious king and illustrious prophet? Once you come to the realization that Aaron's beard with its oil is an allegory for your beards, you should be eager to interpret David's saliva-covered beard allegorically in order to judge your own. Observe how this great man was thought to be some low-born madman, and presented himself as such before Achish, a prince of this world, with the result that he appeared truly despicable and contemptible. With a humiliating sordidness (that is, his saliva) he defiled his wisdom and virtue (that is, his beard), yet the impurity of the saliva flowing over his beard, under the guise of a foolish frenzy, miraculously preserved the purity of his heart, which consists in the beauty of wisdom. Consider carefully, brothers, how your beards are prefigured in the beard of the divine David, and see to it that what was first illustrated in his beard by a seemingly sordid disgrace occurs in yours. Saliva will indeed flow over your beards if with wisdom and patience you endure the sordid humiliations that befall you.

Consider how what was transferred from the allegorizing David to the allegorized David, who represents the Lord Jesus Christ, has at last passed to you. The virtue and wisdom of the Lord, befouled by foolishness and weakness as if by a stream of saliva, humbles itself in the eyes of his followers. Mocked and derided, it became *contemptible to men and was despised by the people*[25] when it endured spit upon the beard and blows upon the cheek. So you, too, *should suffer fools gladly, since you yourselves are wise.*[26] *You will accept it if someone strikes you in the face*, if someone pulls your beard, *if someone causes you loss or takes from you,*[27] because you transform what is weak and foolish in the eyes of God into your own dishonor and shame,[28] since what appears weak and foolish in a beard covered with saliva is in fact braver and wiser than men. Often you mock laypeople by saying, "What a long neck, how round and fat it is—how very nice it would be to give this fat pig a good slap!" Woe to such shameful, bug-filled beards! Flames will devour these beards, which deserve to be burned. Woe to these beards infested with vermin, woe to these beards defiled with streams of saliva, beards worthy of spit and curses, rightfully condemned to burn! Among those who say such things is someone who says, "If only I were allowed to pull that beard, I'd debeard that man, yank out the hairs from the roots and toss his beard into the flames, and when it's nothing but ash and cinder, I'll blow it all away into a gust of wind!" Doesn't someone who says such things appear insane and is thought to be mad like David, whose beard was covered in saliva? Listen up, brothers! Imitate holy David and your life is judged madness, but the real madmen are those who rage in their mockery of your beards and in their mockery never cease to rage. These wretches will stop mocking your beards when their own beards are *burned as fodder for the flames*.[29] And then, when they come to recognize their madness and reconsider your wisdom, they'll lament the tribulations of their spirit and say to you, "*These are the ones we've long held in derision and considered examples of indecency. In our lack of understanding we judged their life to be madness and their end without honor,* and *the sun has not risen for us* (that is, recognition of the truth). *Behold how they are counted among the sons of God, and their lot is among the elect.*"[30] This is Achish, believing David mad and in a frenzy. The name Achish translates to "how is it," by which is meant the ignorance of one who marvels at the Word but does not recognize its truth.[31] This is fulfilled among the Jewish people as well, who didn't recognize Christ when they saw him.

Chapter 8. *How David's beard and the saliva flowing over it relate allegorically to Christ, offered as an example for imitation*

The meaning of the saliva streaming down David's beard as he feigned madness is revealed by the apostle when he says: *The Jews require a sign, the Greeks seek wisdom, but we preach Christ crucified, scandalous to the Jews, foolishness to the gentiles. To those called Jews and Greeks, Christ is the power and wisdom of God. For what is foolish to God is wiser than men, and what is weak to God is stronger than men.*[32] Saliva signifies weakness, but since what is foolish to God is wiser than men, note that saliva is offensive, but observe how it flows over the beard. For as there's weakness in saliva, there's power in the beard. Thus, he concealed his power with his physical weakness, and because outwardly he was weakened, as represented by the saliva, his divine power, like his beard, was hidden within. Behold what a marvelous allegory—the impurity of the beard caused by the flowing saliva conceals, like his beard, his inner purity, and this is the divine power of beauty, virtue, and wisdom! You too, who wear your beards as manly adornment, if you wish to be wise, first be foolish, so that afterwards you become wise when the saliva ceases to flow over your beards and nothing weak or foolish can be seen in it.

Chapter 9. *The vice which causes saliva to flow over either a beard or beardless flesh*

It's also rather remarkable how saliva streaming over a beard is interpreted as impurity when there's no doubt this flow is instead a sign of an infirmity that's recognized as a particular characteristic of youth. Yet streams of saliva in conjunction with a beard aren't a feature of a young age, only streams of saliva without a beard are. It's no surprise that saliva can be found in the beards of decrepit old men, since at that age an abundance of the phlegmatic humor creates a nasty discharge or flow, causing old men to develop catarrh (an unusually excessive discharge is a symptom of catarrh). There are some, however, who from the onset of adolescence constantly suffer from this ailment and are commonly called *bavi* or *bavosi*.[33] Even though a beard is something good and a gift of nature, and saliva, which is also one of nature's goods, serves a necessary purpose for beards, when there's an excessive flow of saliva, the excess brought on by this ailment is considered an impurity. For saliva flowing over the beard isn't something normal, but a corruption—in the natural order of things, saliva is either swallowed or spit out. Job apparently suffered from this disturbance in the natural order when he says to the Lord: *Will you never spare me, nor release me, that I may swallow my spit?*[34] If he were able, he would prefer to swallow the saliva whose excessive flow defiles his beard, something perhaps caused by his weakness. But it's not surprising that someone who scraped off pus with a potsherd seemingly endured the impurity of saliva flowing over his beard, since, what's even worse, he lay down in a dung heap and was covered from head to toe.[35] I hope, brothers, that your beards will be found free of all impurity and preserved unharmed from any burning.

SERMON II
THE FORM OF BEARDS

Chapter 1. *Different styles of beards and moustaches*

But listen, dear brothers! Just as you should keep your beards clean, so should you also keep them properly styled. Some men take delight in having a beard twisted like a rope and a moustache[36] with pointed ends, while others tend to stroke their beard and smooth it with their palm or twirl their moustache with their finger-tips. Some glory in the size of their beard when it reaches down to their stomach, often gazing at it intently as if it were a painting. Yet others shape their beard into branches, and out of a desire to make it look beautiful separate it into a series of little horns, following the fashion of the city. Others trim their beard in the military style, and forgetting their pious country ways hope their beard's beauty makes them look like city-dwellers or curials.[37] If they should ever notice that their military beards don't at all look good when the area around the ears is clean shaven, they would be embarrassed how they make a mockery of themselves by creating a monstrosity out of two opposing styles. Some shape their beard into a sharp point, like the teeth on a saw,[38] or if someone wants to compare such beards to something else, he can admiringly look upon them as pruning hooks. Others groom their beard into the shape of a raven's tail—a bird needs its tail to help it fly, and beards of this kind seem to aid flights of fancy! Men with such beards readily and easily direct all their actions to pleasure. There are also men who have forked beards; sometimes they stroke one half, sometimes the other, and seem to make two beards out of one. We see others who've shaved off their moustache completely, and their bare and pale lips make them look like young boys or women, though their beards prove beyond any doubt that they're men. To have no moustache at all is an abomination that clashes with a beard, for nature has bestowed moustaches onto beards as their natural ornament. But those who want to have an extremely long and full moustache deserve to be criticized, since such a monstrosity disgraces their beard—especially since their moustache drinks from their cup as much as they do! Moreover, men who curl their beards like a woman's hair and desire a beard adorned with a woman's dainty ringlets are strangers to our life of piety. Leave the art of hair curling to little girls' locks, for a curler shouldn't touch a man's beard! Beards that that have been curled should be abhorrent to men who follow the religious life, since not even a layman should affect womanly manners.

And so, brothers, avoid all the vices of the beard I've just listed and style your beards following the Order's regulations: a beard shouldn't hang down more than two fingers below the chin, nor should it be curled up at the sides and spread out as if to make handles, making the beard look wider than it is long. It's better if your beards look like they've been neglected out of rustic coarseness rather than styled into some lewd shape with excessive fastidiousness. But don't let your beards, contrary to all dignity, become dirty or disgust onlookers with their filth. Moustaches shouldn't be shaved off, but trimmed to a moderate length, not so close to the nose that its exhalations cause them to look wet and not so long they hang over the mouth and sink into your cup when you drink. As I said before, moustaches shouldn't be shaved off entirely, which is grotesque, and it's likewise extremely loathsome when laymen completely shave off their beards and keep only a moustache. This style is a frightful monstrosity—a man turns himself into a woman on his lips and chin. Whoever isn't ashamed of depicting both sexes in a one person with a single beard is guilty of creating a hermaphrodite.

Chapter 2. *The partially shaved beards of David's messengers and the meaning of this shameful incident*

Hanun, king of the Ammonites, ordered the beards of David's messengers to be shaved in half and their clothes ripped to their buttocks, and this incident, as is well known, caused them shame and great embarrassment. It's written in the scriptures: *So Hanun seized David's messengers, shaved off half the beard of each, cut off their garments in the middle at the waist, and sent them away. When David was told, he sent to meet them, for the men were greatly ashamed. The king said, "Remain at Jericho until your beard has grown, and then return."*[39] If you take careful note of the circumstances in which this shameful act occurred, you'll realize that evils often arise from good things done imprudently, and evil men return evil for good while good men strive to return good for good. Clearly this is what happened between David and Hanun, since the wicked man disgraced the messengers of the good man by commanding that their beards be shaved in half and their clothes be torn to the waist. Being wise and mature, as their beards indicated, David's messengers act in accordance with the good of obedience. But once they become involved in secular affairs after they're sent to one who loves this world, they're ensnared and fall into confusion, and though they'd been sent out in the guise of wise men, they return as fools deserving of mockery. Heed this warning directed at you, brothers, and take good care that nothing indecent like this happens to you. All of you have been sent as messengers for the good of obedience. All your actions should arise out of necessity and discretion, and the work you do out of obedience should have nothing superfluous or trivial about it. Certainly, those among you whose monastic way of life is believed to be holy and praiseworthy, and is proclaimed as such, possess a beard that remains whole. Suppose a man who lives in accordance with the rule of obedience should somehow become depraved under the devil's influence, but the signs of his monastic vow aren't removed completely—some will realize he has fallen and affirm it, while others remain ignorant of his fall and deny it. The beard of such a man does not maintain its integrity, but because there's disagreement about him, he's guilty of having lost half his beard. The part that represents honor and wisdom is cut off by those who know his sin and affirm it, while the part that represents beauty and virtue is preserved by those who know his error and defend him. But if a fall into ignominious disgrace is so obvious that it can no longer be disguised or defended, half of his clothes are torn to the waist. It's the sin of fornication in particular that gives rise to this scandalous condition, as shown by the reference to the private parts next to the buttocks being exposed.

Chapter 3. *The interpretation of "remain in Jericho until your beard has grown"*

But if there are any among you—God forbid!—whose beards the devil has perhaps shaved in such a shameful manner, we say to them what David said to his men: *Remain in Jericho until your beard has grown, and then return*. Those whom the devil has thrown into confusion must by necessity remain in Jericho until their beards grow back—that is, they're a shame and disgrace before their betters and declared an anathema to all until through good effort and the grief of penitence the outward beauty of their beards (which is the growth of virtue) is reborn and they're considered worthy to be in the presence of their king and his house[40] (that is, his abbot and his fellow brothers). Since Jericho means "moon"[41] and the moon grows smaller over the course of its monthly phases, to remain in Jericho until the beard grows means to mourn the loss of virtue until the beard returns to its original state. But if shaving half a beard is shameful and a half-shaved beard is subject to mockery, how much ridicule is produced by shaving it off completely, at least for whom it's neither permissible nor proper to have no beard at all on account of the Rule of the Order and its teachings?

Chapter 4. *Why the devil is said to shave part of the beard, but the Lord is said to shave the entire beard*

It's worth noting that when the beards are shaved in half the devil is said to do the shaving (as King Hanun shaved the beards of David's messengers in half), but when the entire beard is shaved off, the deed is attributed to the Lord. Thus the following in Isaiah: *In that day the Lord will shave with a razor hired by them that are beyond the river, by the king of the Assyrians, the head and the hairs of the feet and the entire beard.*[42] Nevertheless, since in the case of shaving the beard there's mention of the razor with which the Lord shaves the beard, it could be said without contradiction that, since the Lord shaves the entire beard, he shaves half the beard. For if *there is no evil in a city which the Lord does not cause,*[43] then wherever the sins of man require it the Lord inflicts punishment proportional to the guilt. The Lord destroys what appears to be beautiful and strong, and he shaves in part or whole (that is, he shaves either part of the beard or the entire beard). But the razor the Lord uses to shave is either the devil or a man through whom he inflicts his wrath, as is the case with the king of the Assyrians and the king of the Ammonites. One of them the Lord uses like a razor to shave half the beard, and the other the entire beard. The entire beard is shaved off when men become effeminate through the loss of strength, beauty, and wisdom. There's a prophetic denunciation of such men in another verse: *On all their heads shall be baldness, and every beard shall be shaved.*[44] Many among you are bearded and some are bald (though perhaps more are starting to go bald). Someone who's bearded ought to be educated in the allegory of the beard, and in the same way those who are bald or going bald should know what the scriptures say about baldness or going bald. For it's well known that instances of beard-shaving bear meaning in regard to both good and evil, and likewise baldness is an indication of virtue and vice.

Chapter 5. *Why monks shave their beards but lay-brothers don't*

And why would we shave our beards when you don't shave yours, unless the reasons why we have them and the explanations of their meaning have demonstrated that we should shave ours but you shouldn't shave yours? It's good that we shave our beards and it would be bad if we didn't, just as it's good that you don't shave your beards and it would be bad if you did. Perhaps you'll then ask why we shave our beards and you don't shave yours, and why in each case it seems to be good, even though having a beard and not having one seem to be contraries. Understand that that my response to this will concern faith and morality. The possession and deprivation of a beard (that is, having a beard and lacking one) is the passing of the law into grace. The law was behind a veil and covered, as it were, by a beard; grace, however, removed the veil of scripture and shaved off the beard covering it, as the Apostle says: *When you pass over to Christ, the veil will be removed.*[45] Thus, the law is made manifest through you, who don't shave your beards, while grace is proclaimed through us, who shave them. And since the law isn't destroyed by grace but fulfilled by it, the fact that we shave our beards doesn't eliminate or destroy your ability to have them. Rather, what your possession of beards (which are, in a manner of speaking, veils) signifies is fulfilled in the deprivation—the shaving—of our beards (which is like removing the veil) and is made manifest by revelation. You are the people, with a beard and without a crown;[46] we are the clergy, with a crown and without a beard. In our case, the possession of a crown is the absence of a beard, and in yours, the possession of a beard is the absence of a crown. To put it another way: for you there's a double possession of hair and beard, and for us a double deprivation of both hair and beard. And as the double possession of hair and beard among you veils and conceals the mystery of faith, so the double deprivation of hair and beard among us reveals and lays bare the hidden secret of faith.

Chapter 6. *Moral analogies in the possession or deprivation of hair and beard*

In regard to morals, there's a meaningful symmetry in the presence or absence of hair and beard among both you and us. You perform works of the flesh to sustain and support the needs of the old man, as your hair and beard signify, while our spiritual efforts strengthen the new man in the spirit,[47] and thus we cut away from ourselves anything superfluous, symbolized by shaving the head and beard. You keep your hair and beards and don't shave in order to make ready the things of the outer world, which ought to be objects of ridicule rather than desire; we shave our head and beards in order to acquire through intensive self-examination the things of the inner world so that we can share them with you. These are the things we ought to enjoy together for eternity, because in this lifetime you work for us as well as for yourselves. By shaving our scalp we create the image of a crown upon our head, and when we shave our beard we make bare our chin [*mentum*] in our striving for perfection in mind [*mente*] and spirit, eager to cut away anything unnecessary and earthly from our will and desire. You don't create the image of a crown upon your head and don't shave your beard, because in his simplicity a layman, who's occupied with earthly labors, doesn't possess the education to delve into spiritual matters. Sunk under the weight of the lowliest concerns, he cannot rise to the study of spiritual perfection and reach loftier matters with a mind and spirit lightened of its burdens. Without a beard but with a crown, we sow spiritual seeds for you and reap the harvest of your works of the flesh, because with your beards and your hair you labor for us. Exposed to heat and cold outside, you have your hair and beards as a defense, while we, shut inside for our cloistered way of life, don't feel the absence of hair and beard and have no need of them as you do. Finally, note that beards aren't suitable for the office of the altar, which is our work, while beards aren't incompatible with but, in fact, are well-suited for agriculture, which is your work. We who approach the holy of holies cut away the beard's hairiness, while you who set out to tend the fields show by the possession of a beard that labor is your concern. Think how offensive to the eyes it would be if bearded men wore albs or chasubles! It would be indecent for a beard to hang over books or chalices, and so without beards we tend to the altars and chalices, and you with your beards are assigned to the plow and hoe. So in conclusion, know why you keep your beards and don't shave them, and why we don't keep our beards but shave them.

Chapter 7. *The beard of Ezekiel, shaved and divided into three parts*

Authority together with reason teaches us that we should shave our beards and fashion crowns upon our heads. Indeed, the Lord says to the prophet Ezekiel: *And you, son of man, take a sharp sword that shaves hair and run it over your head and your beard.*[48] If this prophetic shaving of the head and the beard is compared with the previous instances of beard-shaving as a similar allegory for God's judgement, indignation, and wrath, you'll find it's a divine rebuke against the unbelieving transgressors of his law and our Rule as well as against corrupt morals. You'll also find the appropriate punishments, weighed out according to the quantity and quality of the sins and measured out to each individual from the same scales of equity and justice. For after the Lord said to the prophet: *Take a sharp sword and run it over your head and your beard*, he immediately added: *and take a balance for weighing and divide them* (that is, the hairs). He continues: *A third of the hairs you shall burn with fire inside the city, another third you shall cut with the sword round about the city, but the other third you shall scatter to the wind. Then you shall take from these a small number and bind them in the hem of your garment. From these you shall again take some and throw them into the fire and burn them with fire; out of this will come a fire against the entire house of Israel.*[49] Fear the judgment of God, brothers, you who shave neither your beards nor the hairs of your head: *The judgments of God are a great abyss.*[50] It's easy to fall into the abyss, but who can leave it? Be careful and preserve your beards, lest their shavings be made into this fire, which you should realize will without a doubt happen to you if you neglect your Order and find yourselves dismissed from it. Regarding God's punishment of the deceitful vow taken by those who by living in a disordered and dissolute manner violate their Order, it is said: *He sent against them the wrath of his indignation, indignation and wrath and tribulation, afflictions sent by evil angels.*[51] If you're found to be disobedient, to be grumblers and faultfinders, then you grow a beard to your great shame, because not a hair will remain that won't be shaved. And when all the hairs of your beard or head are shaved off, they'll be placed in a scale and divided into three parts: the first part will *be burned as fodder for the flames,*[52] the second will be cut up, and the third scattered. And what else could placing the hairs in a scale mean except increasing the weight of the punishment to balance the amount of sin? And again what does it mean to divide them into thirds if not to match the type of punishment to the type of sin?

Chapter 8. *Why a third of Ezekiel's beard is condemned to burning*

How great do you think the sin is that's punished or purified with fire? How shameful is the offense that's punished by a fire that creates a stench or burns inwardly without light? From which comes the verse: *You shall make them a furnace of fire.*[53] Let the intemperate and unclean, the shameful and foul, whose beards are signs of their sacrilege and fuel for the fire, hear this and tremble. Where shall they be burned? *You shall burn them,* he says, *inside the city.* That is, you shall command them to be burned in view of the people. Read the end of Isaiah: *Their fire,* he says, *shall not be extinguished and they shall be an abhorrent sight to all flesh.*[54]

Chapter 9. *Why one third of the beard is cut with a sword*

And a third part you shall cut with a sword. Those who cut are themselves cut, those who cause schisms and stir up scandals in the community are the very ones who cut into and tear apart unity. The beard-hairs of such men are cut by the *sword of the spirit, which is the word of God.*[55] Observe the cutting: *I wish those who trouble you would be cut off!*[56] Also: *And I will cut down his enemies before his face.*[57] After the cutting he adds scattering: *And I will turn to flight those who hate him.* Someone cuts with a sword if he says: *Drive out the wicked person from among you.*[58] And since *the wicked walk round about,*[59] the hairs of their beards are cut *round about the city,* because *outside are the dogs*[60] who bark and bite, tearing apart the brothers who live in unity. Woe to the beards of those who don't rejoice to hear: *How good and pleasant it is when brothers live together in unity!*[61] Woe to dry and dirty beards, onto which the oil on the head does not flow, the oil that flowed down onto *the beard, the beard of Aaron!*[62]

There follows in the prophet:

Chapter 10. *What it means for a third to be scattered to the wind*

And another third you shall scatter to the wind. This third part of the hair and beard seems to signify flighty and fickle men who are carried away by the winds of excitement, driven along by every temptation. They're compared to dust and straw because of their levity and instability, for they're *like the dust that the wind carries away from the face of the earth.*[63] They're the ones whom God makes like straw exposed to the winds or like hairs shaved from the beard and scattered to the wind. You can see how well this third part of the hair applies to the third kind of monk or lay-brother, who's called a *gyrovagus* in the Rule of our holy father Benedict.[64] It's clear that such men, with their shaved beards or tonsured hair, are shaved and tonsured to their shame and ignominy. Their tonsure is evidence they're lying to God and their lack of a beard demonstrates they are soft and effeminate. However, those whose beards are unshaven and whose hair isn't cut into a crown have something to fear as well, namely the coming of a contemptible baldness or a disgraceful shaving of the head and beard, in accordance with the warning of Isaiah, who prophesied about the Moabites: *On every head is baldness, every beard is shaved.*[65]

Chapter 11. *The origin of shaving or not shaving the beard and the reasons for it, with examples*

The ancients shaved their heads and beards in times of grief and affliction, and thus Job fell to the ground with a shaved[66] head. You can also read about Euphemianus in the life of his son, Saint Alexis: *His father Euphemianus, when he heard the words from the scriptures, fell to the ground in a faint and upon rising cut his garments and began to tear the white hairs from his head and to pull out his beard.*[67] Aedesius, too, the priest of idols and father of the virgin Saint Justina,[68] is said to have shaved his head and beard as a sign of his conversion and penitence. For there it is written: *Then Aedesius shaved his head and his beard.*[69]

And as to the veneration the beards of the pious ought to receive, the monks who would rather mock than revere your beards should take heed of Saint Simeon's beard, for in his life is the following: *But the bishop of Antioch wanted to remove some of his beard and at once began to dry his hands.*[70] Therefore, having a beard, which you wear as a sign of piety and a mark of wisdom and strength, shouldn't be an annoyance or a burden to you. For among the other signs of his piety, the apostle Bartholomew was distinguished by the sign of his beard so that the Indians who wished to know him could recognize him. And when their god Astaroth could make no sign to them since he fell silent in the presence of the apostle, they consulted Berith, the demon of the neighboring city, and spoke to him: *"Give us a sign," they said, "so that we may find him, since we cannot recognize him among so many thousands of men." In reply the demon said, "Curly black hair, pale skin, large eyes, straight and symmetrical nose, ears covered by his hair, long beard."*[71] You might raise a question about his ears covered by hair and his long beard, and ask why you bare your ears by cutting your hair and don't grow a long beard, in contrast to the practice of the apostle, who's said to have ears covered by hair and a long beard, not trimmed as you trim your beards. If you ask me this, I in turn ask you why you don't have wives to keep you company like the apostles did, and also why when crossing fields you don't pluck ears of grain to rub and toss in your mouth to eat, or even why you don't eat with unwashed hands as the apostles did?[72] I say to you that a change in the times requires a change in manners, and the meaning of such changes as well as the explanation of their meaning can be found in the individuals involved and the reason for the changes. And since *everything has its season*[73]—different things please different people and various things are appropriate for various people—, there's a time for growing the hair and beard and a time for cutting and shaving them, according to what's demanded of different individuals and what's indicated in the explanation of their meaning, either as allegorical revelation or moral instruction.

To return to our interpretation of beards, possession of a long beard isn't always matched with good men (or only good men), since we find that evil men have also had long beards. We thus find that an angel of the Lord revealed that the demon Astaroth had a long beard, when it is said: *Then he showed to them a huge Egyptian, blacker than soot, with a narrow face and long beard.*[74] But those who are bearded and coiffed in insolence are condemned to public mockery and the private shame of a diseased soul. Baldness strips away the ornaments of eloquence from their heads, which remain barren and ugly, and when they declare themselves wise, they look foolish. And if because of their beard they seem to possess some manly strength, it's proven to be effeminate and weak when shaved off by a man of the church.

Chapter 12. *What it means to bind a small number of hairs in the hem of the prophet's garment*

The fourth verse of the prophet says: *And take from these a small number and bind them in the hem of your garment.* There's something strange and obscure about this treatment of the hairs of the beard and the head in different ways, a scarcely intelligible riddle—Lord God, explain this parable to us! Holy Spirit, good, or rather best, teacher, reveal this prophetic riddle to your students! Who or what is this small number of hairs from the prophet's beard and head? What does it mean to bind the hairs in the hem of the prophet's garment? How deeply hidden under the obvious literal sense is the allegorical meaning! What shall I say about the garment? We find a garment mentioned in different places in the scriptures. In Isaiah, a *garment of praise* is given *instead of the spirit of grief*, just as *a crown instead of ash* and *the oil of joy instead of mourning.*[75] There's also the garment of Elijah, which fell away from him when he was taken up into heaven, and the garment of Boaz, which Ruth asked to be spread over her, and in Isaiah the short garment, which *cannot cover both.*[76] Each garment is distinguished by its particular characteristics, and in the garment of Ezekiel the hairs of the beard are bound up, but only in the hem and only a few of them. And this is relevant to the present issue of our brothers' beards, which we want to keep far away from any burning, unless we could find a way for our brothers' beards to be burned in the proper way without upsetting them.

When the prophet is commanded to separate the allegory of the shaved hairs' condemnation into the three-fold judgement of burning, cutting, and scattering, he reveals that *many are called* but condemned to punishment.[77] But when he's commanded to bind in the hem of his garment a small number of the hairs from the beard and the head, this indicates that *few are chosen*, but since they're firmly and steadfastly bound to their faith and the grace of divine protection, they're kept apart for their salvation. Thus *who endures until the end will be saved*.[78] For a garment such as this is woven by *faith working through love*,[79] and its hem is the end of their enduring. But if being bound in the hem of this garment is preservation for salvation, it's remarkable that immediately following the prophet is told: *And from these you shall again take some and throw them into the fire and burn them with fire.*

Chapter 13. *The meaning of the fire coming out of the beard hairs cast into the fire*

If those bound in the hem of the garment are kept apart for their salvation, why are some of them taken up and cast into the fire to be burned, unless, as was said above, they're condemned to judgment? The words immediately following seem to confirm this: *Out of this will come a fire against the entire house of Israel.* What does the fire coming out against the entire house of Israel mean, if not that it's burned in its entirety and condemned in its entirety to the most severe punishment by fire? But this is a good fire, a fire that the Lord sent upon the earth, wanting it to burn fiercely, about which he himself said: *I came to send fire upon the earth, and what do I wish if not that it burn?*[80] In a plea for this fire, Isaiah says to the Lord: *If only you would tear open the heavens and come down, the mountains would crumble at your presence, melt as if burned with fire, and the waters burn with fire.*[81] And so, because God is *a consuming fire*,[82] if he kindles the fire of his love in our hearts, that fire comes out *against the entire house of Israel*, since the house of Israel is the hearts of those who look to God.

If, however, it's argued that it's not a good fire that comes against the entire house of Israel from the small number of hairs commanded to be bound in the hem of the garment, on the grounds that this is what a literal reading of this prophetic passage seems to affirm, it's still possible that it says something allegorically about the repudiation and condemnation of the Jews. In fact, the Lord speaks about them in a later verse: *Because they rejected my ordinances and did not walk in my statutes.*[83] He also says to this wicked people: *Behold, I am coming against you and I myself will execute judgments among you in the sight of the gentiles. Because of all your abominations I will do to you what I have not yet done, and the like of which I will not do again. Therefore, fathers will eat their sons in your midst, and sons shall eat their fathers. I will execute judgments on you, and all of you who remain I will scatter to every wind.*[84] All of this, which, as is clear, happened to the Jewish people before the coming of the Lord, is represented symbolically in the shaving of the hair and beard and in the burning, cutting, scattering of the hairs. But the son of God, born from that people, chose a few of them, the small number of hairs from the beard and the head, which is to say the apostles and some other disciples, and taking them under the grace of his protection and faith, he bound them in the mystery of the new law, as if in the hem of his garment, until the *end of consummation.*[85] But he then took some from among these few and threw them into the fire and burned them with fire, which happened when they went back after saying: *This teaching is difficult, who can listen to it?*[86] And Judas, one of the twelve, betrayed him, so he cast him into the fire when he dismissed him with a just judgment according to his *heart's desire,*[87] saying to him: *What you are going to do, do quickly.*[88] Ablaze with feverish greed, Judas kindled the flames of avarice, from which arose a fire against the entire house of Israel when he was eager to sell and all the Jews were burning to buy. Notice, brothers, how the prophet Ezekiel's beard was dispersed: part to burning, part to cutting, part to scattering, and again in the fourth verse a part to burning.

Chapter 14. *The prophet's beard should be a warning and a sign for the beards of the lay-brothers*

But if the beard of such a great prophet was shaved and condemned to burning for the sins of others, what do the beards of those men deserve, who without any regard for their own faults knowingly and intentionally stir up a storm that makes shipwrecks of men's souls? This is, in fact, what I said in the other letter: "The beards of those who knowingly and intentionally stir up a storm that makes shipwrecks of men's souls should *be burned as fodder for the flames!*"[89] If you cultivate your beards with wisdom, I think you'll respond to this curse in a single voice: "So be it, so be it!" Indeed, because you love peace and truth,[90] the anathema of burning won't harm your beards. So now call back to mind the beard of the prophet Ezekiel, and let his beard, which was sentenced to numerous punishments for the crimes of others, serve as a warning to you so that your beards, as their own particular source of sin, aren't grown to create confusion and aren't condemned to the punishment of burning

Also note carefully how this prophet always remained the same, both before, when he was growing a beard, and after, when he'd shaved his beard. In this interpretation, we and you are one and the same, since before, when he wasn't shaving his beard, he followed the custom of lay-brothers, who don't shave their beards, and then later, when he shaved his beard, he was a prefiguration of the monastic Rule. Finally, you shouldn't be troubled and complain about why you're called lay-brothers or why you don't shave your beards, since both reason and authority have demonstrated this is how it should be.

SERMON III
THE NATURE OF BEARDS

Chapter 1. *First observation on the nature of the beard*

There's still another aspect of the nature of beards we should examine, so that, just as we've learned about the character of faith and moral doctrine from the presence or absence of beards, we can also admire in them the craftsmanship of nature, or rather give glory to the craftsman of nature, by whose wisdom a wondrous and praiseworthy power is made visible in the form of beards. In this regard, our first observation is that a beard distinguishes one sex from the other (men from women), since by nature men possess beards, but women don't. However, it does happen, albeit rarely, that men are made beardless and women have beards.

Chapter 2. *Second observation on the nature of the beard*

Our second observation is that for the same sex (male), at one age it's natural to have no beard at all, while at another, it's natural not to be completely beardless, unless this occurs because of an inborn defect or an accident. It's appropriate for infants and children not to have beards at their age, while for the remaining ages (namely, mature adults and the elderly), once the beard begins to sprout in adolescence, nature directs that they shouldn't be without beards, unless, as I already said, either an inborn defect prevents it or some accident suddenly removes it.

Chapter 3. *The circumstances in which men don't have beards or lose them*

An inborn defect creates an obstruction to beard growth when from the time of conception until birth males develop such a frigid constitution that some of them are unable to know women[91] and they remain beardless until the end of their life. Beards are lost accidentally when, after the genitals have been cut off either surgically or in an act of violence, men are either deprived of the beards they otherwise would've had or the beards they already had subsequently fall out completely or become very patchy.

Chapter 4. *The difference between the habits of the beardless and the bearded, and a moral comparison of the individual types*

Because they're beardless, eunuchs (whether they came to be naturally or artificially) aren't distinguished from women by a beard, and for this reason they should make sure they don't become unlike men in their morals, since they're not actually women. Otherwise, they'll be included among the effeminates for their lack of a beard as well as for their unmanliness in imitating women. Likewise, full-bearded men should make sure their full beards don't falsely represent them as men in the case they're found to be unmanly and effeminate. Partially bearded men, however, who are commonly called *raspagi*, stand at the midpoint between unbearded and fully bearded. They're no longer beardless but haven't become fully bearded—no longer beardless, but just barely, and not close to being fully bearded. Beardless and fully bearded differ in terms of "none" and "much": as beardless is non-bearded, fully bearded is much-bearded. By this logic, beardless men are non-bearded in the same way full-bearded men are much-bearded. The partially bearded, however, who exist midway between beardless and fully bearded, should avoid becoming monstrosities by combining male and female, since they're neither beardless nor fully bearded. Because they're not fully bearded, they seem to be less than men, but because they're not beardless, they can still be called men. When they're fully masculine, the partially bearded are far different from the beardless and remain close to the fully bearded. However, when the partially bearded are weak and unmanly, they're very similar to the beardless but are separated by some distance from the fully bearded. If the fully bearded are fully masculine, their glory is both external and internal, while for the beardless, if they lack manliness, there's confusion and disgrace both outwardly and inwardly. Yet of the two incomplete types, it's better to be beardless and manly than fully bearded and effeminate. The partially bearded should strive to be manly in order to imitate fully the fully bearded, and should avoid becoming soft and effeminate, since otherwise they'll receive the same mockery for their partial beards that the beardless receive for their beardlessness.

There are yet other distinctions drawn among beards, such as the ex-beard, the early beard, and the late beard, and these distinctions correspond to the characteristics that define ex-bearded, late-bearded, and early-bearded men. Ex-bearded men are both the same as and different from the beardless. Insofar as they're the same, there are overlaps between them, since ex-bearded men are beardless and there are beardless men who are ex-bearded. Insofar as they're different, there are oppositions, since there are beardless men who aren't ex-bearded, just as there are ex-bearded men who aren't beardless. In terms of the oppositions, the beardless are so by nature, the ex-bearded by artifice. As to the overlaps, those simultaneously beardless and ex-bearded are so by nature and artifice. Nevertheless, "ex-bearded" implies artificial rather than natural, "beardless" natural rather than artificial. For "ex-bearded" [*eberbium*] means to become without a beard [*extra barbam*] after having a beard, which happens artificially, and "beardless" is to be without a beard, which is natural. Those who shave their beards (that is, those whose beards are shaved) are ex-bearded by artifice, women are beardless by nature, and eunuchs are simultaneously beardless and ex-bearded by nature and by artifice. As to the fact that young boys are naturally beardless because of their frigidity and women are naturally beardless because of frigidity, in the case of young boys, their age precludes them from being ex-bearded and they transition from beardless to beards naturally, while in the case of women, nature keeps them beardless their entire life.

Chapter 5. *On the unnatural beards of women such as Galla*

Nevertheless, there are cases of women who, contrary to nature, have had beards. In his *Dialogue,* Saint Gregory tells of a bearded woman named Galla and explains why she had one.[92] After some preliminaries about the beard and its cause, he adds: *Because there was an extreme build-up of fire in her* (that is, Galla's) *body, the doctors told her that if she didn't return to a husband's embraces, she would, contrary to nature, have beards because of the excess of heat.* Galla is said to have "beards" in the plural, not "beard" in the singular, a usage that derives from the scriptures, which frequently use the plural for the singular and the singular for the plural. For just as here "have beards" is said instead of "have a beard," so too in the examples above "of beards" is used in the plural for "of a beard" and "beards" is used for "beard." In the first example: *So Hanun seized David's messengers and shaved off half of their beard.* Note "of their beard" for "of their beards," the genitive singular for the genitive plural. And the second example: *Remain at Jericho until your beard has grown.*[93] Here we have "beard" for "beards," nominative singular for nominative plural. Galla was one woman and had a beard, not beards, and in the same way, men in the plural don't have a beard, but beards. However, when the doctors said that contrary to nature she would have "beards," this doesn't mean that the doctors find fault with or criticize nature (for they're investigators and defenders of nature), but there's no question that the doctors said that it would be contrary to nature (that is, opposed to the usual course of nature) for this woman to become bearded. For in the case of women, nature causes them not to have beards from a naturally inborn coldness, while in the case of Galla, nature caused her not to remain beardless, as is usual with other women, because of an accidental excess of heat and instead she grew a beard. And though in the usual course of nature to have a beard is a source of honor and beauty for a man, to lack a beard is a source of honor and beauty for a woman. And contrariwise, to remain completely beardless is a source of ugliness and shame for a man, while for a woman to be bearded is a disgrace and an outrage. But Galla preferred to avoid the embraces of a husband and keep her beard rather than abandon her vow of chastity and, by remaining beardless, give honor and glory to impure flesh. And thus she is described in that passage: *But this holy woman, who loved the beauty of her inner spouse, feared no outward ugliness, nor was she ashamed if something her heavenly spouse did not love in her made her outwardly loathsome.*[94] This woman, brothers, is the best example for men, since she wasn't ashamed of her beard because she loved its creator. If any among you has a face that is less attractive because he's beardless or partially bearded and fears the mockery of others, he should emulate Galla, the bearded woman, who was not ashamed of a face disgraced by a beard. Since she wasn't ashamed of her beard, he should follow her example and, rejoicing in his inner beauty, feel no distress because he's beardless or partially bearded.

However, the description of Galla as having plural "beards" rather than "a beard" can be understood in a way different than was proposed. Plural "beards" could mean fully bearded, and so to say that Galla had "beards" means only that she was fully bearded. Indeed, a woman who looks fully bearded would seem to be more grotesque than one who looks only partially bearded. And since "partially bearded" covers three types of beards, when all three are present at the same time it's perfectly reasonable to describe someone who has all three types at the same time as having "beards," so that "to have beards" means fully bearded.

Chapter 6. *The three types of beard included under "partially bearded," plus a fourth type*

There are, then, three types of beard: on the chin, under the chin, and on the jaws. Sometimes the beard is on the jaws but not on the chin or under the chin, sometimes it's under the chin but not on the chin or on the jaws, and sometimes on the chin but not on the jaws or under the chin. Anyone who recognizes them and has seen them can bear witness to the truth about these types of beard. On the day I began to write this sermon, I saw (and preserved in my memory) a beard that was only on the chin and not on the jaws or under the chin. The one who provided the evidence for this type of beard was a brother named Ogerius, who was bearded on the chin and not on the jaws or under the chin. Each of you should take a look at his own beard and, if he finds that he's fully bearded, he can ponder the other types if he wishes. But if he finds that he's partially bearded, he can learn what type of partial beard nature has either enriched him with or left him poor and destitute of. There's also a fourth style of partial beard, found on the jaws and on the chin and under the chin, but with hairs sparsely scattered. This type isn't included under full beards or under the three types of partial beard.

Chapter 7. *On the play of wisdom with nature, not only in beards but also in other things*

In all these beards are clearly present wondrous nature as well as praiseworthy and joyous wisdom. Because of the joy it brings, wisdom is described as "playing" not only in the varieties of beards but in every kind of thing, playing before God and playing in the world. Wisdom playing before God as nature is something for angels to contemplate and rejoice over, while wisdom playing in the world with nature is a source of wonder and joy for mankind. For this reason, Wisdom herself[95] speaks about playing with nature in forming together with God all things through nature, in nature, and with nature: *When he set the foundations of the earth, I was with him, forming all things, and I was delighted every day, playing before him, always playing in the world, and my delight was to be with the children of men.*[96] *I was delighted*, she says, *playing*: this is wisdom's delight from playing in the works of nature, especially in those related to men, because her *delight was to be with the children of men*. Who's unable to recognize in beards and beardlessness both the work of nature, at which we ought to marvel, and the play of wisdom, glorious in its joy?

Chapter 8. *Why men laugh either rightly or wrongly about the play of wisdom in beards or in other things*

All play causes laughter and all laughter contains joy. Men thus laugh about beards and beardlessness on account of the play of wisdom, but some laugh joyfully to the praise, honor, and glory of wisdom, while others laugh jokingly, increasing and spreading foolishness. Wise men find joy in laughter but don't engage in mockery, while fools joke around with laughter and engage in mockery. Sara laughed at the play of wisdom with nature when fertility was promised to her in her barrenness,[97] but Sara laughed with joy, giving birth to laughter, the child of her joy—that is, Isaac, named from his mother's laughter (his name means "laughter").[98] Some foolish boys laughed at Elijah's baldness and mocked his bald head, saying: *Go away, baldy! Go away, baldy!*[99] But because they mocked the work of nature as well as the working and play of wisdom, all those who laughed at his baldness were mauled by two bears. It's the same with beards: fools mock the work of nature and the working and play of wisdom with nature when they mock the beardless and the partially bearded. When fools see fully grown or elderly men who are beardless or women who are bearded, they laugh at the work of nature and mock the working and play of wisdom with nature. But since wisdom teaches and instructs us through its working, it's in works of nature that it illustrates nature allegorically, then uses allegory to create teachings, and uses teachings to form and develop morals according to the monastic Rule.

I included this discussion in order to draw from these three types of partial beards (on the chin, under the chin, and on the jaws) their allegorical or moral meaning, in praise of wisdom and to the glory and wonder of nature.

Chapter 9. *The moral interpretation of the mentanea beard and the submentanea beard (that is, the beard on the chin and the beard under the chin)*

What is the chin [*mentum*] if not the sharpness of the mind [*mentis acutum*]? And what is the sharpness of the mind if not a sharp mind [*mens acuta*], one that has been sharpened [*exacuit*] by wisdom? And what is the beard on the chin if not wisdom inhabiting a sharp mind? The beard under the chin [*sub mento*] is called *submentanea*, in the same way the beard on the jaws [*maxilla*] is called *maxillaris*. The beard under the chin is a lower beard, and the beard on the chin is a higher beard; the beard on the chin, because it's higher, is wisdom about divine matters, and the beard under the chin, because it's lower, is wisdom about human matters. To have a beard on the chin is to go beyond the mind for God by contemplation, while to have a beard under the chin [*sub mento*] is to be sober [*sobrium*] for men through compassion. Thus the saying of the apostle: *If we go beyond our mind, it is for God; if we are sober, it is for you.*[100] *If we go beyond our mind, it is for God*—this is the beard on the chin; *if we are sober, it is for you*—this is the beard under the chin.

Chapter 10. *On the goat's beard, with a thorough discussion of its great mystery*

There's another quite wondrous thing about the beard under the chin that we ought to discuss. Indeed, I wonder, but can't wonder enough, why a goat is bearded along with all its offspring and why nature gave a beard to no other species of brute animal except this one. As you all know, this species has a beard, but only under the chin. But who can reveal the hidden causes of nature, since, at it is written, *nothing is done in this world without cause?*[101] But divine mysteries lie hidden in the secret causes and in all of these is found the play of wisdom with nature in the world. Who will unravel this knotty question for us, so that we may know why only this species of brute animal resembles man in the common trait they share, having a beard? Yet this similarity is of such a kind that there's a double dissimilarity in it: first, a beard occurs naturally in both sexes of goat, but in the case of humans, only males have beards by nature; and second, this animal only has a beard under the chin, while it's a natural characteristic of men to have a beard on the chin, on the jaws, and under the chin, at least in the male sex and at the appropriate age for a man to have a beard. Age is no obstacle to a goat's beard—it appears bearded as soon as it's born, if it's going to have a beard at all.

If we're ignorant about nature and the reason why this is the case, we should be eager to examine this figure from nature as an allegory about faith or a moral teaching. This animal holds a place of great significance in the holy scriptures, since it represents the figure not only of the sinner, but also of the Savior. Accordingly, both sexes of this animal rightfully have a beard, since the Savior, who was sacrificed in the form of this animal as a prefiguration of and testimony to the law,[102] created both sexes, male and female, and thus also comes to redeem and save both. This animal therefore rightfully has a beard, because it prefigured both the wisdom made flesh that had to be sacrificed on behalf of sinners and the wisdom of the world, which the wisdom of God makes foolish.[103] And since in his capacity for reason and wisdom man was created in the image and likeness of God,[104] when this resemblance to the divine was lost through sin, man fell into a state similar to animals, in which only the wisdom of the flesh could be found in him. This is what the beard under the chin [*sub mento*] of this brute animal illustrates. For since by his sin man fell away from the wisdom of the divine mind, when he lost this state of mind he could know nothing except what was beneath the mind [*sub mente*], which is to say, in the flesh. And the goat is a prefiguration, set forth as a sign to the sinner so that by its stench and the beard under its chin he may recognize how displeasing to God is the uncleanliness of the sinner and the wisdom of the flesh, which is hateful to him.[105] And since all this creates a stench before God, there is the command to sacrifice the goat so that it's transformed into the odor of sweetness when sacrificed for the Lord.[106] However, in its resemblance to sinful flesh, a goat is an allegory of the Savior, since the beard under its chin symbolizes wisdom made flesh and corrupted. Its sacrifice can be understood to mean that he who had no sins of his own suffered on the cross for the sins of others. Moreover, the fact that this animal is bearded as soon as it is born seems to convey, in accordance with it as an allegory of a sinner, that not even an infant whose life on earth lasts but a single day is without sin,[107] since to be born in sin is shameful to the same degree that an infant born bearded would be disgraceful and monstrous.

Yet another interpretation could be offered: because the beard symbolizes virtue and wisdom, this animal, since it's already bearded from birth, indicates that man in his original state is endowed with virtue and wisdom and gifted with a manly maturity. A man should thus carefully consider that when he's tormented by both his sin and the punishment for his transgression, this animal is an image of him because he suffers from his fall and struggles to recover and because he's eager to unburden himself of what he's forced to bear. He should endure his punishment and cleanse himself of sin by the sacrifice of this animal, and he should strive to return to virtue and wisdom by thinking about his own beard. He should contemplate why Jacob, on his mother's instruction, eagerly hastened to prepare the two best kid goats for his father, who gladly ate them,[108] since the conversion of sinners is a delightful and welcome repast for the Savior. The wise mother gave her son clever and wise instructions when she told him the meal should be prepared only from bearded animals, and in this way taught him that with one of the goats the virtue and wisdom of God would be sacrificed, and with the other the sinner would be cleansed of sin by punishment and return to the understanding of truth and the love of virtue, and this was indicated by the beards of the goats. And one goat was an example for the other: the one in pain but without sin was an example for the one in pain and with sin, just as it was said: *Christ suffered for you, leaving you an example that you should follow in his steps; he committed no sin, nor was deceit found in his mouth.*[109]

There was also, as the law informs us, an emissary goat, which was sent into the desert instead of being sacrificed,[110] because the Jews asked that Barabbas be released to them, and he was a foul-smelling goat whose beard, similar to theirs, represents not wisdom but insane foolishness. And when they say, "We don't want Christ released, but Barabbas,"[111] they're out of their mind [*mente*], they become mindless [*amentes*] and, as if bearded under the chin [*mento*], they transform themselves into foul-smelling goats, since they chose to save the life of a stinking goat but condemned to death a spotless and sweet-smelling goat. Nor does it seem irrelevant to the teaching of truth that the emissary goat symbolized Christ's divinity. The pain of death was foreign to it because it could feel no suffering, but the other goat, which was sacrificed, symbolized the humanity which suffered death in Christ because he took on flesh.

We, however, don't follow the darkness of the Jews, but walk in the manifestation of truth, so let's leave to them the bearded goats and bulls and horned rams and the law's other cloaks, under which the sluggish and sleepy Jew sleeps. A goatish beard hangs beneath his chin and covers his chest, cloaking his heart and preventing him from understanding the truth. The Jew is thus mocked by all, since, as I said, a goat's beard hangs beneath his chin and he doesn't understand the great mystery of divine mercy which was *made manifest in flesh* and *raised up in glory*.[112] The Jew sacrifices a goat so his beard becomes greasy and his gullet's stuffed full; his understanding isn't illuminated with an allegory of the truth, but (to use coarse language) his beard grows thick from the fat he belches up. The Jew's stomach swells and his belly grows fat from devouring *goats with the finest wheat*, he becomes drunk, and his mind's senses are deprived of intellectual sobriety from *drinking the purest wine from the blood of the grape*.[113] In mockery the Jew is called "goat's beard," because with a perverted mind opposed to wisdom's understanding his beard is under the chin and not on the chin.

Chapter 11. *The beard on the jaws and various explanations of its moral meaning*

The *maxillaris* beard, which covers both the right and left jaws and adorns both cheeks, still remains to be discussed. First, we will examine if there's anything sinful in this style of beard, so that anyone bearded in this manner will know what to avoid. The form of this beard is in fact disgraceful and monstrous, since it's neither on the chin nor under the chin, but appears only on the jaws. Some men want to look wise and prattle on about things they're ignorant of, though they have disgraceful thoughts [*mente*]. Their feminine chin [*mento*] is a renunciation of masculine beauty, and like those without a beard under the chin, they attract the eyes of admirers with their whorish allure. Indeed, these men prostitute their lustful and venal charms in the same way whores use the beauty of the throat beneath the chin to inflame the desires of their shameful lovers. This is why Solomon declares that in the lustful gaze of the man she's seducing a concubine's throat gleams more than oil[114]—this part of the body wouldn't arouse any desire if there were a beard under the chin. A beard of this type, only on the jaws, most often appears on those who are starting to mature and have recently reached puberty, an age that gives birth to the beginnings of lewd behavior and creates the foundations for the shameful life to follow. In fact, as soon as a growing young man passes from beardlessness to the beard growth of puberty, he should abstain from the wanton behavior caused by sexual desire so that the seriousness that comes from maturity will emerge together with his beard in the same way that capriciousness earlier accompanied his beardlessness. In wearing his beardlessness as a sign of inconstancy and wantonness, a beardless adolescent or young man makes excessive use of the liberty allowed his age and by his pursuits and behaviors ably demonstrates the truth of what Horace says: *Beardless youth, with his guardian finally removed, rejoices in horses.*[115]

However, in scripture jaws metaphorically refer to learned men,[116] and when one comes across men who are all talk and no action, a partial beard of this type (only on the jaws and not on the chin or under the chin) marks them out for disgrace. They produce words with their jaws, the only place they have a beard, but they don't have prayers in their mind, because those who during prayer don't go beyond their mind [*mente*] for God don't have a beard on their chin [*mento*].[117] They don't have beards under their chin [*sub mento*] because they aren't sober [*sobrii*] for those they teach, to whom they show neither care nor compassion. On the other hand, someone who goes beyond his mind for God through prayer (which is having a beard on the chin) say to him: *In me, God, are your prayers that I will return, praise for you.*[118] He also says: *I will return to you my prayers, those that my lips uttered.*[119] What prayers? *I will offer to you burnt offerings rich in fat, with the smoke of sacrificed rams.*[120] *Burnt offerings rich in fat*: the prayers of the mind, the mind I go beyond for you by contemplating you; *with the smoke of sacrificed rams*: leading the flock with the ardor of grace by being sober for followers, showing them care and compassion. Also, *I will make an offering of bulls together with goats.*[121] *Bulls*: plowing up the hardness of your heart until the harvest of patience; *together with goats*: by *crucifying the flesh together with its vices and lusts,*[122] since the goat that's been sacrificed has a beard under the chin.

A beard is in a fully-bearded state if it has the following forms: on the jaws, on the chin, and under the chin. According to the scripture's teaching, a beard on the jaws possesses patience and consolation, just as it possesses both sides of the jaw, and it proclaims that we should place our hope in these: *Whatever was written was written for our instruction, so that through patience and the consolation of the scriptures we might have hope.*[123] On the left side is patience, on the right consolation, so that this beard is known to adorn both cheeks. Or the beard on the jaws occupies both jawbones, where the molars are located, because someone who teaches eats both for himself and for those he teaches. Someone eating for himself is told: *Sacrifice and eat;*[124] someone eating for others: *Break your bread for the hungry;*[125] someone eating for both himself and others: *You who inhabit the land of the south, meet the fugitive with bread.*[126] Jeremiah laments over those who, because they eat for themselves and not for others, have a beard on the jaws that's shaved in half: *The children begged for food but there was no one to give it to them.*[127] Related to this is what Ezekiel says: *Woe to the shepherds who feed themselves but do not feed their sheep.*[128] According to the interpretation offered above, the beard on the jaws has a left half and a right half corresponding to the bread of grief and the bread of consolation. The bread of grief is barley-bread and the bread of consolation is the bread of angels, which man eats.[129] Elijah ate the bread of consolation under a juniper tree and, *strengthened by this food, walked for forty days and forty nights to Horeb, the mountain of God.*[130] The beard on the jaws also signifies strength, because a great many men were slaughtered with a jawbone: Samson is said to have struck down a thousand men with the jawbone of a donkey and killed them all.[131] If someone reminds us that the jawbone used as a weapon for battle came from an animal that doesn't have a beard, this is no obstacle to our interpretation of this beard, since there's no doubt that in the holy scriptures this animal symbolizes strong and persevering men, for whom it's a natural characteristic to have a beard. In fact, Isacar was called a *strong donkey* by his father,[132] and though his beard is nowhere mentioned, it's impossible to believe that he didn't have one. For how could Isacar be called strong in praise of his manly reputation if he showed any signs of feminine softness or effeminate behavior? In response to this question of strength, which a beard on the jaws signifies, it's enough to mention the doubled jawbone, which has both a right and left side: strength knows neither what it's like to be broken by adversaries on the left nor what it's like to be exalted by the prosperous on the right. Anyone who knows how to *live in prosperity and to endure poverty* like the apostles has adorned both sides of his jaw with a worthy beard. And as for anyone who when *struck on one side of the jaw offers the other*,[133] the beard on the jaws, which adorns and beautifying both sides with a sign of manliness, demonstrates that he's a strong man.

Chapter 12. *A beard as a sign of five things, all of which should be equally present so that neither the sign nor the beard is deceiving*

A beard properly adorns a man in every respect when it's a sign of beauty, a sign of strength, a sign of wisdom, a sign of maturity, and a sign of piety. And when these are all equally present in a man, he is rightly said to be fully bearded, since the beard, appearing in full on the chin, on the jaws, and under the chin, proves that he's fully a man and not some half-man or she-male. But if a beard, in its capacity as a sign, doesn't correspond to the five manly goods mentioned above, it's a deceiving sign. The sign is a lie and so is the beard, which clearly deserves to be set ablaze, *burned as fodder for the flames*.[134] Listen, brothers, and pay close attention to the following analogy about the beard as a sign, and you'll know how to prevent both the sign of your beard and the beard itself from being deceiving. A barrel-hoop is placed in front of a house or tavern as a sign of wine and signals that there's wine in the house or in the tavern. If there's wine in the house or tavern, it's a true sign and directs those seeking wine to find it. But if wine isn't in the house to which the sign is affixed, it's a false sign, deceiving those in search of wine, and is subject to the anathema of burning, because it sends away empty-handed those weary from searching. Observe that it's the same with a beard, about which a long sermon has already been delivered by this "barbilogist" (meaning someone making a sermon about a beard [*barba*]). And what is a sermon about a beard if not a "barbilogy"? Anyone who reads this barbilogist's barbilogy carefully should recognize that it's divided into three separate sections: on the cleanliness of beards, on their form, and on their nature. And in these sections he also shouldn't fail to study everything connected to the allegory of faith and to morals.

Chapter 13. *On the nature of the early beard and the late beard*

Not everything that a careful inquiry can discover about the nature of beards has yet been said. In fact, even though above I treated at length the nature of the partial beard, the full beard, and beardlessness, when I included mention of the early beard and late beard, I failed to add anything further about them.[135] But so it doesn't seem like I'm passing off my ignorance as knowledge, when I claimed to have discussed the nature of the beards I first mentioned, it wasn't because I had thoroughly examined the causes and explanations of each one (something about which, in fact, I'm ignorant), but because in the course of delivering the sermon I described what happens in accordance with nature and the natural order (about which I'm not at all ignorant). For who doesn't know who the early-bearded and the late-bearded are, and that it's something that happens naturally? And again, who doesn't know that younger men often grow beards before their elders, just as they often have gray hair before their elders? Which is why someone once said: *unseasonable gray hairs are scattered over the head.*[136] Among those whose beards arrive early, some glory in their new condition, while others are embarrassed because a beard seems unseasonable at their age. Similarly, among those whose beards come late, some find it distressing because they're afraid of mockery, while others rejoice because they want to keep looking young. Those who suffer from embarrassment because their beards come late often smear honey or some other ointment on their chin and jaws, or sometimes they even shave to stimulate beard growth. In the same way, men ashamed of their gray hairs will use a red dye on their hair, because they would rather look redheaded than gray. Yet among all these men the ones who deserve ridicule are those who, when they're a little older, blame nature when *gray hairs* that aren't *unseasonable are scattered over the head.* However, some men whom nature, contrary to its normal course, covers in gray hairs before their time, attempt to thwart nature by cloaking their natural hair color with an artificial one. But perhaps they can be excused somewhat for doing this, since their age seems to suffer an injustice, in that an age at which gray hair is inappropriate has gray hair, just like when an age at which a beard is inappropriate produces a beard. If a beard arrives before adolescence, it's an early beard; if the beard's arrival is delayed until after adolescence, the proper term is late beard. Those whose beards come in adolescence shouldn't be called either early-bearded or late-bearded, unless either the beard grows excessively thick at the end of puberty or it's still too patchy at the onset of manhood. Finally, those whose beard refuses to grow even at the end of manhood will still remain beardless afterwards.

Chapter 14. *The interpretation of the early beard and late beard for faith and morality*

Like the other kinds of beards, early beards and late beards have something to contribute to the interpretation of faith or morals. Those who make early progress in acquiring good judgment are adorned with an early beard, while those found to be sluggish and lazy, whose indolence makes them dull-witted and faint-hearted in receiving moral instruction, are rightly called late-bearded. Nevertheless, if God should not forsake them when they finally reach a ripe old age,[137] they wouldn't then continue to be foolish old men, but at an age suitable to acquiring wisdom they would by some miracle begin to be wise, just as it would be miraculous if even at that age their beard would first begin to grow.

Chapter 15. *How the beard serves as a sign of beauty*

As a sign of beauty, an early beard benefits some, but harms others. If deformities such as spots or blotches appear on someone's chin or under his chin or on his jaws, he needs an early beard to mask these ugly marks under a beard's covering. Anyone suffering from gout needs a beard that's extremely thick and long, since this is a deformity beneath the chin. But if someone has a chin that looks deformed because it protrudes too far or is disproportionately thin, he also needs a beard to cover it. But if someone's jaws are defiled by extremely unseemly splotches or are distended in an undignified manner, he needs to cover his face with both an early beard and a full beard. Finally, faces with wrinkles or clusters of warts need the cover of a beard to serve as a sign of beauty. If these deformities are innate, an early beard is needed; but if they arise after a time by chance, a full beard is always required, even if an early beard is not needed in every case. An early beard seems to harm only those whom a beard causes to look much older than they are and is thus a source of embarrassment. Indeed, a vice nearly everyone has is the tendency to argue back and forth about differences in age, with someone always wanting to look younger than (or not as old as) someone else; a dispute arises about beards and gray hair with some claiming their gray hairs are "unseasonable" and their beards came too early. The beardless are excluded from this dispute, since it's acknowledged that on account of the circumstances and causes I mentioned much earlier they remain forever without a beard. But they can console themselves with the fact that they've dispensed with the bother, effort, and pain of shaving a beard—or at least those have who are required by the Rule to shave their beards, provided there is, in fact, a beard that can be shaved.

Chapter 16. *The beard as a sign of strength*

The beard is useful as a sign of strength if there's strength corresponding to the sign of the beard. For if someone whose beard makes them look handsome is soft and effeminate, he's like Diotrephes, whose name is interpreted to mean "insane beauty."[138] The common proverb, which goes "a handsome man is a corrupt man," strips him of his beauty, since he's feeble and soft even though he bears in his beard a sign of strength. For *in vain does the crippled man have beautiful legs,*[139] and so too does the soft and depraved man wear a beard in vain, and just as the presence of beauty in a crippled man's legs would obviously be not to his glory but to his shame, so softness and depravity render a man adorned with a beard deserving of our rebuke.

An example of this is Mephibosheth, the son of Saul, who, though endowed with a beard as a sign of strength, was said to have limped on each foot,[140] a sign of weakness and depravity. He's described as follows: *Mephibosheth, the son of Saul, also came down to meet the king with his feet unwashed and his beard unshaven.*[141] (Mephibosheth is called the son of Saul because he was the son of Jonathan, the son of Saul.) His unwashed feet and unshaven beard are mentioned to show his contemptible character and ignominious lowliness, while the limp of his weak feet proclaims his powerlessness. In the same passage, it's said he also didn't wash his clothes in order to show that he had given himself over to negligence completely, with his feet unwashed, his beard unshaven, and his clothes neglected in filth. Therefore, when Mephibosheth is described in this way, on a literal level he's vile, contemptible, and disgraceful; interpreted allegorically, he's praiseworthy and good; interpreted morally, he's reprehensible and detestable. Finally, his name, which means "indecency from the mouth" or "shame of the mouth,"[142] fits all these interpretations if carefully applied in each case. For what is vile, contemptible, and disgraceful is shameful to speak and indecent to utter from the mouth—namely, to meet the king with unwashed feet, an unshaven beard, and clothes neglected in disgusting filth. This is the literal meaning. But on an allegorical interpretation, it's praiseworthy that a lowly outcast in this world goes to meet Christ the king—the lame meets the upright, the weak the savior, the unclean the cleanser, and the needy the dispenser of all goods and riches. And someone who was the subject of a disgraceful and shameful tale on everyone's lips and in everyone's ears became in the end a king's dinner guest, his feet washed and beard shaved, dressed in costly garments and crowned with glory and honor.

But if on the basis of his perverse behavior (unwashed feet, unshaven beard, and unwashed clothes), Mephibosheth is interpreted morally, his unwashed feet are unclean desires, his unshaven beard is the wisdom of the flesh overflowing with vanity and not cut off from filthy profit-seek-ing, and his unwashed clothes are sordid deeds. In daily life, these are exposed to the censure of all and become the subject of scornful remarks, and thus Mephibosheth, to whom disgraceful things are attributed and shameful things ascribed, is "indecency from the mouth" and "shame of the mouth." For why else would this Mephibosheth be called Meribaal (that is, "disputing with the Most High") in the Paralipomenon[143] if not because someone of perverse morals *resists what God has ordained*[144] and is always opposed to the divine and supreme will, which is to dispute with the Most High? What else then could it mean for Mephibosheth or Meribaal to have an unshaven beard if not that he's daring beyond his own strength and virtue and disputes with the Most High? And what good is it for Mephibosheth to have an unshaven beard as a sign of strength when he himself is lame and weak? Let's listen to the man himself when he con-fesses to his lowliness and weakness. When king David asked him: *Why did you not come with me, Mephibosheth?*, he answered: *My lord, O King, my servant had contempt for me; for I, your servant, told him to prepare a donkey for me so I could ride it and go with the king, because I, your servant, am lame*, but he refused.[145]

You see then, brothers, that it isn't good to meet Christ the king with an unshaven beard. So shave your beards following the decree of the Or-der. Otherwise, if your beards remain unshaven, they will grow to excess and begin to teem with vermin, as is said to have happened to the manna when it was gathered in excess.[146] For if "everything in excess becomes a vice," then on account of vices, which are vermin, your beard shouldn't re-main unshaven, just as the manna shouldn't have been gathered in excess, because it then begins to teem with vermin.

Chapter 17. *By what reason or authority beards are commanded to be trimmed or not trimmed. just as they're commanded to be shaved or not shaved*

There is, however, an explanation of the reasons and circumstances for trimming or not trimming beards, just as there is for shaving them or not, and this, as you have already heard, is determined by authority and reason. In fact, in Leviticus there's something you've not yet head about. A person cleansed of leprosy is ordered to remain outside the tabernacle for seven days, to which is then added: *On the seventh day, he shall shave all his hair: head, beard, and eyebrows, all the hairs on his body.*[147] Here's the source of the hidden mystery behind the command to shave the beard! In a later passage of Leviticus, which says: *You shall not practice augury nor interpret dreams. Neither will you cut your hair in a circle,* there immediately follows: *nor shave your beard.*[148] What a remarkable thing—in the earlier passage there was a command to shave the beard, but here shaving is prohibited! In the first instance, since the disease had been cured, there was a command to shave off the beard insofar as it is a sign of strength, because someone who has no health or strength in himself shouldn't take on anything beyond himself. The reason for the instruction to shave the eyebrows after the beard is to show that it's only out of pride that someone puts confidence in his own strength or power. Eyebrows [*supercilia*] represent pride, which is the beginning of all sin[149] and at the same time the queen of vices, and this is why the haughty are called "supercilious." Thus someone said: *Put away your your pride* [*supercilium*] *if you acknowledge you're a friend,*[150] as if to say, "Shave away the pride in your eyebrows [*supercilio*] if you want to have the sociable life of a friend." Then you'll also shave your beard, because you you won't think yourself handsome or strong or wise.

The second verse from Leviticus—*neither will you cut your hair in a circle nor shave your beard*—seems directed at us, but in such a way that one of the two commands (not to shave the beard) applies to you, while the other (not to cut the hair in a circle) concerns us, and so for both you and us the verse seems contradictory. However, the spiritual meaning applies to both you and us, provided we live in the spirit and not in the flesh.[151] The hairs of the head are the thoughts of the mind, and the world is round and because of its roundness is called an orb. Therefore, we don't cut our hair in a circle if we don't conform our thoughts to this world, following the saying of the apostle: *Do not conform to this world.*[152] Nor do we shave our beards if we don't despoil our souls of wisdom. This, brothers, is what not shaving the beard means. Take care that it applies to you both outwardly and inwardly.

Chapter 18. *The beard as a sign of strength (Augustine)*[153]

Just as the oil on the head that flowed down onto the beard, the beard of Aaron, that flowed down onto the hem of his garment. What was Aaron? A priest. Who is a priest if not someone who, when he didn't find in the world [*mundo*] something pure [*mundum*] to sacrifice, sacrificed himself? But the oil came from the head. Christ is our head and the holy spirit comes from the head. Where does it go? To the beard. A beard signifies strong men, a beard signifies grown men, energetic men, eager and active. And when we describe such men, we say, "He's a bearded man." And so that oil first descended onto the apostles, descended onto those who endured the first assaults of the world, and thus the holy spirit descended onto them. And those men who first began to live in unity also suffered persecution, but because the oil had flowed down onto their beard, they suffered—they suffered, but were not conquered. Indeed, preceding them in suffering was the head from which the oil flowed down onto the beard, and with such an example before them, who could overcome their beard?

Stephen was sanctified because of such a beard. To not be conquered means charity is not conquered by the enemy. Those who persecuted the saints thought they were victorious—they killed, the others were killed; they slaughtered, the others were slaughtered. Who wouldn't think that the first group were the conquerors, the second the conquered? But because charity was not conquered, oil flowed down onto the beard. Look at Stephen: charity raged inside him, raged against them when they listened to him, and prayed for them when they stoned him. What did he say when they were listening? *You stiff-necked people, uncircumcised in heart and ears, you are forever opposing the Holy Spirit.*[154] Observe his beard: did he flatter them at all? Did he fear them? Because oil flowed down from his head onto his beard, charity was not overcome. Oil flowed down from his head onto his beard because as he was being stoned, he knelt down and said: *Lord, do not hold this sin against them.*[155] And so the apostles were like a beard, for many of them showed strength and suffered many persecutions. If the oil had flowed down onto the beard in vain, we wouldn't now have monasteries. But because it flowed down onto the hem of his garment (for the verse says: *that flowed down onto the hem of his garment*), the church then succeeded and gave birth to monasteries from the Lord's garment. For the priestly garment is a symbol of the church, the same garment about which the apostle says: *That he present to himself a glorious church, without a spot or a wrinkle.*[156] It's cleansed in order to be spotless, it's stretched out in order to have no wrinkles. On what does the fuller stretch it if not on a cross? Everyday we see tunics crucified in a way by fullers, crucified in order to have no wrinkles. What then is the hem of the garment, my brothers? What are we to understand by the hem of the garment? The hem is the end of the garment. How are we to interpret the end of the garment? Is it that the church will have brothers living in unity at the end of time? Or from the hem are we to understand perfection, because the garment is brought to completion by the hem? Those who know how to live in unity are perfected, those who fulfill the law are perfected. How then is the law of Christ fulfilled by those who live in unity as brothers? Listen to the apostle: *Bear your burdens in turn, and in this way you will fulfill the law of Christ.*[157] This is the hem of the garment. How, brothers, are we to understand which hem is meant, onto which one does the oil flow? I don't think the hem along the sides is meant (for there are hems on the sides). But the oil could flow down from the beard to the hem that's at the head of the garment, where there's an opening in the tunic. Those who live in unity are such that, as a man's head enters through those hems in order to clothe himself, so Christ, who is our head, enters through brotherly concord in order to be clothed, so that the church cling fast to him.

Chapter 19. *The beard as a symbol of wisdom*

As was shown above, a beard is a sign of beauty and a sign of strength, but it's also a symbol of wisdom. And taking wisdom into consideration, even though a beard shouldn't be shaved, it shouldn't remain untrimmed either. For having an untrimmed beard is nothing other being wise in a high-minded manner. *Do not be wise in a high-minded manner,*[158] he said, which is to say, "trim your beard." *Do not be wiser than you ought to be, but be wise in moderation.*[159] That is, don't let your beard go untrimmed. Someone who disputes with the Most High (like Meribaal) is wiser than he ought to be; he produces disgrace from his mouth and does not hide the shame of his mouth (like Mephibosheth). Therefore, brothers, trim your beards, so that they'll truly serve as a sign of beauty, a sign of manliness, and sign of wisdom. For there are many among you who are bearded in such a becoming manner that the beards themselves shine with a kind of wisdom and wisdom seems to speak through their whiskers. And we rightfully glory in the Lord when we find that in anyone with such a beard there's nothing improper, nothing foolish, nothing contrary to wisdom, nothing opposed to prudence, nothing in harmony with stupidity. On the other hand, we're justified in feeling aggrieved and lamenting that in the great beards of some men we find great stupidity, and we're filled with great shame that cast against them is the common saying "Wisdom doesn't dwell in a beard." What could be more jarring than a fully bearded man who's full of stupidity, who devoid of any understanding of wisdom wants to look like a man of deep understanding, and who with a flourish of his beard tosses around words of utter foolishness? These men overflow with beards as well as words, they're tepid with their charity, inflated with pride, stiff-necked, and armed with a fat neck.[160] How much better it would be for them if they were humbled by a partial beard, or rather no beard at all, and were fluent in their speech and ardent with their charity! As if they're bearded in wisdom, such men are effusive in giving advice, overflowing with judgments, abounding in arguments, rife with rumors, shot through with plots, intricate in their subtleties, and quibbling in their reasoning. In all of this they want their beards, as a sign of wisdom, to make them appear distinguished and venerable. When such men try to defend their views and the opinions they pronounce, they bring forth their beards, as if they were something to be revered, to serve as their witness, so that whatever they assert when swearing on their beards will be treated not as unbelievable, but as sacrosanct. These are the kind of men who say "by this beard, yes" or "no" or "so it will be" or "it will not be otherwise."[161] There's also the type who's so confident that wisdom burns and shines in his beard that in the midst of his pronouncements he stubbornly shakes his beard and, twisting it in his hand, invokes a curse of burning: "May a terrible flame devour this beard if it's not the case" or "if it will turn out otherwise."

You, who swear an oath upon your beard or summon a curse of burning against your beard in order to validate your wisdom by an oath or curse on your beard, aren't you aware that in the Gospel you're prohibited from swearing any kind of oath?[162] Since you're forbidden from swearing an oath by the hairs of your head, because you're not able to turn a single one white or black, why do you dare to swear on your entire beard? If you're not permitted to swear on even a single hair of the beard, how do you dare to put your entire beard under an oath? If the hairs of the beard belong to you and the beard belongs to you, these belong to you not because you have the ability to create them, but only because you've received possession of them. Not a single hair of the beard or the beard itself will belong to you when he who gave them to you so wills. If the beard has been given to you as a sign of wisdom, you shouldn't turn it into an instrument of your stupidity or an insult against your creator.

Chapter 20. *Examples of men whose beard was a sign of wisdom*

The beards of those who understood that they received them as a sign of wisdom remain in our memory, and even after their death their beards are remembered as a distinctive feature. Saint Gamaliel's beard is commemorated as one such example. In the *Revelation of Saint Stephen*, he appears in Lucianus' dream and is described as follows: *I saw*, he said, *an old man, tall, geroprepes (that is, a worthy priest), gray-haired, with a long beard* etc.[163] Note the long beard is mentioned as a description and distinctive feature of a wise man, because if someone is said to have a beard of great size, it indicates he's a man of great wisdom. And Gamaliel was indeed a wise man, learned in the law and the teacher of Paul, who was himself the teacher of the gentiles.[164] When Lucianus asked Gamaliel who he was, he replied: *I am Gamaliel who nurtured the apostle Paul and I taught the law to Jerusalem.*[165] Gamaliel is thus said to have had a long beard as a sign of wisdom because he was learned in the law, renowned for great wisdom, and taught a wise man to be wiser, just as if he had encouraged him to grow his beard. Moreover, that fact that this wise man is said to be gray-haired also refers to his understanding of wisdom, and thus there's gray hair together with the beard, since, as it is written: *Wisdom is with the aged.*[166] This is why the scripture also says: *A man's understanding is his gray hair,*[167] and prudence is the gray hair of men.

Chapter 21. *The beard as a sign of maturity as well as wisdom*

And since a beard is a sign of maturity as well as a sign of wisdom, it's only right that gray hair accompany a beard, since no one, as is known, is endowed with true wisdom unless he also possesses a dignified maturity. A gray beard, as a sign of wisdom as well as maturity, adorns men whose *hearts are cultivated with wisdom,*[168] while on the other hand, old men are rightly judged to be foolish and mad if they're found to possess frivolousness and stupidity along with their gray beards. Young boys judged Samuel and Daniel to be such men. To one of them a beardless boy said: *You old man of evil days* etc.[169] Are his gray hairs and the old man's beard he wore as a sign of wisdom and maturity being insulted, or is the young boy stupid, a false judge, and devious, who stands convicted of his libidinous lust? Concerning men who despite being bearded and gray-haired have surrendered themselves to a debased understanding and have sunk into the filth of debauched foolishness, it was said: *A venerable old age is not a length of time or the number of years counted up, but man's understanding is his gray hair and a blameless life is a mature old age.*[170] Woe to you, whose gray beards flourish while you're still boys in understanding, effeminate in your lewdness and just as womanly as if you were beardless! Why do you disgrace with your silliness and stupidity the signs of wisdom and maturity (that is, your beards and gray hair)?

Chapter 22. *Examples of men whose beard was a symbol of maturity and wisdom*

The examples taken from writings in which mention of beards and venerable gray hair indicates individuals honored for wisdom and maturity—do these have no effect on you? In the life of Saint Gregory we find mention of his father Gordian's beard in a passage describing him, including his clothing and his beard: *Gordian dressed in a brown rain-cloak, with a deacon's tunic*[171] *under the rain-cloak, and wore boots; he was tall, with a narrow face, green eyes, a beard of moderate length, thick hair, and a serious expression.*[172] Wisdom, maturity, and piety all come together in this description: piety in his dress, maturity in his serious expression, and wisdom together with maturity in his beard. But why is his beard said to be of moderate length, since in many cases a long beard is said to be a source of praise, as was the case with Gamaliel above? If his beard is taken as a sign of wisdom, then having a beard of moderate length means to not possess any pompous learning and to be wise in moderation rather than wiser than one ought to be. If as a sign of maturity his beard is described as moderate, it means either to refrain from inordinate care in styling the beard or to cut back its excessive length in order to preserve its cleanliness. For a beard can become moderate by cutting it back in moderation; otherwise, an untrimmed beard could perhaps be harmful by inviting criticism, as was demonstrated above in the case of Mephibosheth (who was severely rebuked for coming before the king with unwashed feet and an untrimmed beard). But if a beard is described as moderate because it's naturally that way, it's possible to relate this to back to the partial beard. But if a moderate beard is declared to be a symbol of piety, this can still be the case by trimming it in a dignified manner, since even when the moustache is shaved off, as was mentioned much earlier,[173] the beard can be trimmed in a pious manner, avoiding the military or city style.

Chapter 23. *The beard as a sign of piety*

This pious form of a moderate beard has been introduced for the benefit of your beards, brothers, so that nothing improper will arise from their excessive length or excessive thickness. For "moderate" implies "humble," and so humility should always be exhibited in a moderate beard so that a beard becomes a symbol of piety in this respect as well. For this reason, one could perhaps bring up the fact that, after Gordian's moderate beard, another man's moderate beard is later mentioned among the many different details about him. For it's said there: *His beard, like his father's, was blond and short.*[174] That is, just as the father's beard was blond and short, the son's beard was pictured as blond and short in a portrait skillfully painted by an artist on a circular fresco.[175] Because a beard is a sign of piety, piety grows in the mind [*mente*] of those whose beard grows on the chin [*mento*]. But just as the beard doesn't grow unless it takes root on the chin, neither does piety grow unless it has been rooted and established in the mind through charity.[176] How I wish the beards of those from whose minds piety has been plucked out, or for whom the beard of piety didn't grow along with their beards, would be plucked from their chins! But the beard of piety couldn't grow because it didn't take root in the mind, just as the beard that doesn't take root on the chin can't grow.

Chapter 24. *The example of the prophet Ezra demonstrates that the beard is a sign of piety*

The pain caused by uprooting the piety planted in the mind is as great as the pain and anguish caused by plucking out the beard from the chin. The prophet Ezra made sure to indicate this when he plucked out his beard,[177] which caused pain to his flesh, because he perceived that piety had been lost, which caused pain to his mind. Sitting down in grief, he plucked out his beard to demonstrate how great the pain in his mind was from pulling up the roots of his beard from his chin: *When I heard*, said Ezra, *those words* etc.[178] Which words, if not that the children of Israel had lost the religion he had preached when, contrary to the law of God they'd received, they married foreign wives, and with pain he saw that they had turned to idolatry in contempt for the observance of the divine religion? Tell us, Ezra, tell us what you did when you pulled out your beard, even though the pain of plucking it out was so great. *When I heard*, Ezra said, *those words, I tore my garment and my mantle, and pulled out* (or *plucked out*) *the hairs of my head and beard and I sat down in grief.*[179] In behaving like a mourner, Ezra revealed the pain deep within his heart: he tore his clothes, he pulled out the hairs of his head and beard, and he sat down in grief, in order that the defilement of his body and his clothes along with the grief on his face would all the more quickly stir everyone's soul to repent their own sin or their brother's. In fact, our clothes usually illustrate our actions: if they're clean, they're to the glory of whoever wears them, but if they're obviously unclean and lack the splendor of nuptial love,[180] they're for death. The hairs of the head represent thoughts, which arise from the roots hidden within our heart as if from the deepest recesses of our mind; if our thoughts are righteous, they should be preserved, but if corrupt, cut away. This is why Samuel's mother said of him, since he was destined for holiness: *And no razor will touch his head.*[181] And the Lord to the apostles: *But not a hair of your head will perish,*[182] because, of course, all the thoughts of holy men are worthy of eternal remembrance before the Lord. But for a sinner to be cleansed of his iniquities, he must cast off his debased thoughts, the origin and source of evil deeds. Thus, in addition to the other ceremonies of purification that followed his recovery, the leper in Leviticus was instructed to shave off all the hairs of his flesh to earn reentry to camp by this sacrificial expiation.[183] For we are completely cleansed of the foulness of our vices only when we make the effort to remove from ourselves not only harmful deeds, but also harmful thoughts.

Moreover, a beard, which is an indicator of a man's sex and age, is often used to signify virtue. The priest[184] tore his garment and tunic to indicate that the deeds of the people he governed were less than perfect, and that through penance these must be torn apart from their stupidity and renewed into whole cloth. He pulled out the hairs of his head to impress upon these people that their vain thoughts must be eliminated from their hearts to make room for the rebirth of useful thoughts. He also pulled out the hairs of his beard to make these people humble even in those virtues they seemed to possess, and to remind them that before the tribunal of our inner judge a virtue that's clearly mixed with vice counts for little or nothing. And he sat down in grief to teach them that forgiveness for such great sin must be earned through the weeping born of repentance.

Take heed, brothers, and be wary of wearing a beard as a sign of piety in vain, else we who are your superiors will perhaps have to grieve over many of you and in our heart's affliction be compelled to do what Ezra signified when he pulled out his beard. For those of you whose beards are still growing because you haven't yet reached a mature age, let wisdom grow along with your beard, which is its sign; let your inner beauty grow, let your strength grow, let your maturity and your piety grow. In this way your beard will prove to be a true sign of beauty, strength, wisdom, maturity, and piety. Therefore, brothers, if you make an effort to progress in these five areas, in the order they've been presented and discussed, you'll truly be lay-brothers and your beards will be blessed, honored with reverence, and worthy of remembrance.

Chapter 25. *The example of two adolescents, one starting to show a beard, the other not yet*

Those whose beards are still advancing (that is, who are beginning to show a beard) and those who aren't yet growing one should take as a model two adolescents, one of whom one is starting to show a beard while the other still remains beardless. The abbot Vindemius tells us that abbot Macarius[185] spoke about them, saying: *Once when I was sitting in Scetis, two young men came to me from abroad. One of them was beginning to show a beard, but the other not yet.*[186] Macarius himself describes what their life and conduct was like afterwards, and I'll let the one who recounted these things for you, brothers, tell the story so that your imperfection can benefit from their perfection. So listen to a little more. Macarius says that he saw demons in the form of flies swarming over the younger, who was beardless: *I saw,* he said, *demons in the form of flies swarming over the younger one, some were trying to land on his mouth, others on his eyes. And I saw an angel of the Lord with a flaming sword defending him and driving the demons away. But they weren't able to come near the older one.* Also, when the beardless younger boy was chanting the psalms, with each verse *a lamp of fire came out of his mouth and rose into the sky.* Likewise, whenever the older one (whose beard was growing) *opened his mouth to sing, a stream of fire like a rope came out of his mouth and reached up to heaven. And I realized,* said Macarius, *that the older boy was perfected, but an enemy was still fighting against the younger.* He concluded: *Come and observe,* he said, *the martyrdom of these two pilgrims.* Behold, brothers, you have heard a miracle astonishing and wondrous, to be praised as well as feared, which seems related to the allegorical understanding of being beardless and being bearded.

Chapter 26. *What a beardless face attacked by flies means*

Notice that these swarming and biting flies attacked the beardless face but were unable to attack the face covered with a beard. Flesh feels pain when wounded, but hair doesn't feel pain even when it's cut; if a fly gets into hair, there's no sensation nor does it cause pain, but a fly climbing over flesh, even if it doesn't bite, creates an annoying sensation and it's an unbearable irritation to anyone trying to shoo it away. This is what that beardless young man, or rather adolescent, seemed to endure, though the other, whose beard was growing, didn't suffer from the flies at all. And this comes as no surprise, since, as you can recognize, the one whose bare mind [*mens*] is still without wisdom, just like his chin [*mentum*] is bare without a beard, is attacked by demons in the form of flies, while the one whose mind is now beginning to be adorned with wisdom, as his chin is with a beard, either suffers less from the attack of the flies, which are demons, or is rendered completely immune from the attack of the flies. Yet it still often happens that flies create some kind of sensation when they crawl over a beard, not because they bite, but because they scurry around on their feet, leading to an examination of the beard solely on account of the irritation they cause by their crawling.

Chapter 27. *The fly of flattery landing on the beard of Amasa*

One of these flies is flattery, which lands on the beard, and if it isn't perceived, it causes death without being noticed. Such a fly landed on the beard of Amasa when Joab said to him: *Greetings, my brother. And Joab took Amasa's chin in his right hand...*[187] Or, as Josephus related, Amasa was held by the beard and stabbed in the stomach with a sword.[188] Then the book of Kings continues: *as if to kiss him*, but he put his left hand on the sword, and *struck him in his side and his entrails spilled out onto the ground and he died.*[189] What does it mean to take hold of the beard or the chin?[190] It's like flattering someone out of kindness. But putting the left hand on the sword and striking the side is to destroy someone with spiteful deceit. Flattery and deceit are such wicked flies! They lead to death unexpectedly—they fly around a man's mouth, infect his beard and chin with their poison, and run from his beard and chin to the spilling of his entrails, which is to say, to his death. When you're praised for your wisdom or prudence, your beard's being held, but beware the one fly of flattery and the other fly of empty glory. In the above passages, there's no real difference between saying held by the beard versus by the chin, except that it seems more prudent to say "chin" rather than "beard," since "chin" refers to both a bearded chin and beardless chin. And although flattery harms both the bearded and the beardless, it usually harms adolescents, who aren't yet growing beards, more than those of a more advanced age, who are progressing in wisdom before God and man.[191] And keeping in mind the proper interpretation of the allegory, this distinction seems to hold true in the case of the adolescents discussed above, the younger of whom, the beardless one, was constantly tortured by demons in the form of flies, but they didn't dare approach the older one, who was growing a beard.

Chapter 28. *The objection that beardlessness wasn't detrimental to the younger adolescent nor did a beard help the older against the flies, followed by a response*

But someone, clearly feeling provoked, says that it wasn't on account of his beardlessness that demons in the form of flies harmed the younger adolescent, since Macarius says that some flies did indeed come to land on his mouth, but others landed on his eyes, a place where a beard that could ward off flies isn't applicable. The implication seems to be that the possession of a beard also didn't help the older of the two against the flies, but rather he could have been attacked in the same spots as the younger, where beardlessness wasn't detrimental, unless some other explanation exists that can be proven with a more valid argument. But someone who's provoked by this doesn't seem to be beardless or a child in understanding, but you'd think he wears a beard as a sign of wisdom! Yet we say that it's one thing to take the proper interpretation of the allegory into consideration and quite another to make every possible connection between things based on outward similarities—it's always foolish and absurd to pursue that course. And if the mouth is often used to mean the entire face or its expression, as in: *He watered his mouths with tears*,[192] this objection thereby loses its force. A beard is still applicable and effective against the flies, while beardlessness is exposed to their biting. And if flies harm the bearded with their excrement, they harm the beardless with their bite as well as their excrement.

Chapter 29. *Why demons in the form of flies landed on the mouth or on the eyes of the beardless adolescent*

Let's consider why in the case of the beardless adolescent some demons in the form of flies landed on his mouth, but others on his eyes. Demons are hostile and troublesome to men in their various vices, which are like the filth and excrement of flies, as was shown in the case of this beardless youth. Because an enemy was still fighting against him, as Macarius testified, he was set apart from the perfection of his companion, whose beard was beginning to show, by some imperfection, just as he was set apart from him in his beardlessness. As long as no beard is visible, an individual's sex can be ambiguous if it isn't indicated by other markers, because a beardless face doesn't indicate male or female. But when a beard begins to sprout, a man is coming to perfection, and then at last, because he grows a beard, he carries in this sign the perfection of a man. In the same way, once he's initiated into wisdom, he eagerly strives for perfection, because it's appropriate to put aside boyish thoughts along with a boyish appearance. In recognition of this, Macarius said: *And I know that the older one was perfected*—that is, the one who was growing a beard as a sign of perfection—*but against the younger an enemy was still fighting*, because he perceived that in his case beardlessness was a sign of imperfection.

Chapter 30. *The flies that attack the eyes or assault the mouth because of beardlessness*

Why is it then that some of the demons in the form of flies landed on his mouth, but others on his eyes? It can only be that through impure impulses and unclean thoughts malign spirits impede the eyes, distorting the vision of contemplation and the gaze of meditation, and obstruct in the mouth the truth of confession and purity of speech. For what are the assorted fantasies and various blasphemous offenses that transfix and defile the mind's eyes during meditation and contemplation, causing our eyes to wander in curiosity, if not the flies through which demons, who are themselves utterly foul, use as their foul instruments in creating temptations?

Chapter 31. *The two ways in which flies prevent confession from the mouth because of beardlessness*

Indeed, the flies that land on or hover over the mouth prevent confession either through the embarrassing shame at the sin's disgracefulness or through the fear of humiliation arising out of an ambition for some honor or high office.

Chapter 32. *The division into nine types[193] of the other flies that are around the mouth because of beardlessness*

Among the flies hovering over the mouth, some bite with slander, some spew excrement and venom with insults and rebukes, some pollute the mouth with jeers and insolent chatter, some defile the tongue with disgraceful language, offensive jokes, or idle worldly talk; some cause distress with gluttony and a stuffed belly, some *set their mouth against heaven*[194] with grandiloquence or boasting, some defile the conscience by excusing faults or, what's worse, defending sin.

Chapter 33. *Which flies hinder prayer or visions because of beardlessness*

But I think no one who prays is unaware of which flies, or rather demons in the form of flies, land on the mouth during prayer. The blind man who in prayer exclaimed: *Jesus, son of David, have mercy on me!*[195] endured flies of this sort on both his mouth and his eyes. Passers-by admonished him to be quiet because such flies were attacking his mouth, while from the other flies swarming over his eyes he'd lost the vision of contemplation (thus his blindness).

I've digressed from the subject of beards only slightly, since this touches upon beards and beardlessness: the flies were unable to come near the adolescent growing a beard but tormented the beardless adolescent in his mouth and eyes.

Chapter 34. *The angel driving away the flies from the beardless adolescent with a flaming sword*

An angel defended the beardless adolescent with a flaming sword, but a sword doesn't seem suitable for driving away flies. Indeed, other things are used to drive them away: there's one that makes a sound to scare them away, for example, or a fan that creates a breeze. However, a sword could still make sense since the angel with the flaming sword was driving away demons, not flies; or, because flies are especially afraid of fire, they became frightened and were forced to flee. But we, too, who preach the word of God to you with the sword of the spirit, which is the word of

God,[196] we drive away flies of this kind from you, so that they dare not land on your beards or attack your mouths or eyes. That sword is *speech purified by intense fire*,[197] such that they're unable to endure the flame of a sword that burns intensely.

Chapter 35. *The lamp of fire coming out of the beardless adolescent's mouth and the flaming rope coming out of the mouth of the newly bearded adolescent*

But also consider, brothers, whether the wonderful double miracle of the lamp of fire and the fiery rope relates to you in some way. Those of you still without beards should strive to imitate the beardless adolescent, from whose mouth the lamp of fire appeared to rise up into heaven, while those of you showing the first growth of beard, or rather with beards already present, should strive to imitate the newly bearded adolescent (that is, the one starting to grow a beard), from whose mouth a rope of fire stretched out to heaven. The monks should note in particular that these marvelous signs happened to these adolescents while they were chanting (that is, during the singing of the psalmody).

Chapter 36. *What the lamp of fire coming out of the beardless adolescent's mouth is*

Do you want to know what the lamp of fire is? Ask a potter.[198] *My heart*, he said, *grew hot within me and during my meditations the fire burned*.[199] And also: *because my heart is aflame*,[200] this lamp ascends to heaven. And since *we have this treasure in clay vessels*,[201] it's rightfully called a lamp. The good of the one who was tempted is represented by a symbol made of fragile clay; his age, still beardless, was also fragile, and the lamp is a vessel which even a slight fall will break. Or perhaps this adolescent, because he was now close enough to the beard's first growth to show a beard, was constantly contemplating the lamp of wisdom in his heart—namely, Jesus Christ, whom Job calls the *despised lamp*,[202] which was first broken and extinguished in death, but then, restored through resurrection, grew strong and ascended into heaven in a bright blaze. During the psalmody, a monk should keep this lamp in his mouth during the act of contemplation, and with a burning and blazing devotion send it into heaven to appeal to the father. This lamp is the one the woman lit to seek and find the coin she had lost.[203]

Chapter 37. *The rope of fire coming out of the newly bearded adolescent's mouth*

Now let's examine the rope of fire that comes out of the mouth of the newly bearded youth (that is, the one growing a beard). Whoever puts into practice what he displays as a sign moves toward the perfection of wisdom. Because a *triple-braided rope is difficult to break,*[204] it's a sign of perfection. If the rope is the holy scripture, it's braided with a triple meaning—historical, allegorical, and moral—, and the holy spirit sets it aflame with the fire of divine love and fiery speech. This rope of fire reaches into heaven, because he who *made the heavens by understanding left nothing intact*[205] that wasn't spoken of in the scriptures, so that whatever is knowable can be known through scripture. In fact, it clearly tells us that heaven itself was made and given order by its lights.[206] The entire rope of fire coming out of the mouth of someone chanting the psalms is set aflame by the love of heavenly beings and reaches to heaven. A further consideration about this rope leads us to find a complete and perfect good in it. *I will tell you, O mortal,* one prophet said, *what is good and what your God asks of you: to do justice, to love kindness, and to walk humbly with your God.*[207] If you practice these three things with a burning heart and use these to praise your God, so that his praise is always in your mouth,[208] the triple-braided rope of fire comes out of your mouth and reaches to heaven. Or the fiery rope is love directed to God with all your heart, all your spirit, and all your mind,[209] because fire is love; or it's a burning desire to be freed from prison, to depart from exile, and to return home; or the rope of fire coming out of the mouth is also the desire in this extremity, when it seeks rest from toil, joy in renewal, and the promise of eternity, seeking these things as it reaches to heaven, in its thoughts and longings dwelling in that eternal country.

The example of the two adolescents, one without a beard and the other showing its first growth, made it pleasant to include in the sermon a bit of a digression on the images connected to them, and those of you long in years or in beard should be ashamed if what you've heard doesn't set the heart within you afire. And as for the rest of the sermon, let's summon the "barbilogy" back to your beards, since it began with them and will rightfully end with them.

Chapter 38. *Invective against those who mock the "barbilogy" or the "barbilogist"*

Perhaps there'll be some people who laugh at this "barbilogy" and mock me with the name of "barbilogist." But I advise them to be careful not to laugh or mock me to their own sorrow for making a sermon about beards, like the children mentioned above who to their own sorrow laughed at Elijah's baldness and to their own sorrow mocked the bald man as he was leaving. Let them mock, if they dare, the beard of Aaron anointed with the oil that flowed down from his head onto his beard, or let them mock the beard of David coated with saliva and the partially shaved beards of his servants, who remained in Jericho until their beards grew. Will they also mock the Lord, who in Isaiah used a hired razor among Assyrians to shave the head and both the hairs of the feet and the entire beard, and against Moab proclaimed: *On every head is baldness, every beard is shaved?*[210] If they laugh about these things or mock them, they shouldn't forget the beard of Ezekiel, one part of which was shaved, another part burned, and a third part scattered to the wind.[211] At the same time, they should also remember Galla, who had a beard. And if someone's beard is either short or long, will they laugh?[212] Gordian's beard is moderate and Arsenius' long, and the description of him gives no one grounds to laugh at his beard: *There was*, it says, *an angelic look to him, adorned with white hair, just like Jacob, elegant, but not luxurious. He had, moreover, an extremely long beard, reaching down to his stomach, but his eyelashes fell out from excessive weeping.*[213] If anyone needs to laugh at a shaggy beard, Esau was hairy and shaggy all over and there's no mention of his beard being smooth.[214] If you read about Mephibosheth's beard in the book of Kings, it's said to be untrimmed, but not shaggy, although Josephus, as we know, described it as shaggy, not untrimmed.[215] Who would laugh, or rather who wouldn't grieve, hearing that the prophet Ezra pulled out the hairs of his beard because of the sins of his subjects?[216] Whoever laughs at the play of wisdom in beards or in baldness should listen to the one who responded: *I, too, will laugh at your destruction!*[217] Didn't wisdom laugh at the destruction of the children who twice shouted *Go away, baldy! Go away, baldy!* in mockery?[218] At the first *Go away, baldy* came one bear and at the second *Go away, baldy* came a second bear; together the two bears avenged the double *Go away, baldy.* The acceptable kind of laughter about the play of wisdom was already discussed above.

Chapter 39. *Who laughs properly at the play of wisdom and who laughs improperly*

Laughter should be accompanied by admiration and joy, not by mocking derision. In Jacob's struggle with the angel,[219] the wisdom of his play offered a wondrous spectacle for laughter, because the loser departed unharmed and the victor was made lame—don't you laugh when you hear this? Jacob accepted his hobbling with a blessing—don't you laugh at the play of wisdom in this? You marvel, you rejoice, you're gladdened, you're consoled—therefore you laugh. There should be the same kind of laughter, not the least bit different, about beards and baldness. But anyone who says to his companion "You have the beard of a goat!" laughs improperly because it's done in mockery. Someone says to another, "Your red beard is a sign of infidelity" and another's rough beard is called a sign of cruelty, and the thin black beard of someone else is "like pitch from hell."

Chapter 40. *The division of beards into four types, their appearance, and their moral equivalents*

Quiet, fools! David was gentle, kind-hearted, and faithful—and his beard was red.[220] Allow wisdom to play with nature in beards, and it will distinguish them, making them different in size, type, style, and color: in size, great or small, long or short; in quality, abundant or patchy, smooth or rough; in style, consisting of one, two, or three parts; in color, white, black, red, blond, or gray. Men with beards of great size should be renowned for the greatness of their souls and be preeminent in their understanding of wisdom; those with smaller beards should strive to adorn with humility that in which they're moderate, even if they themselves are big. As for those who have long or short beards, the former should have long patience in their hope, while the latter should scorn this life as short and of a moment and every day be apprehensive that in a short time they'll depart from this world. Of those whose beards are abundant or patchy, the former should gather in abundance the riches of wisdom and knowledge[221] for their salvation, the latter, if they are patchy or thin in understanding or ability, should strive to compensate with good morals. Of those who have smooth or rough beards, the former should imitate the smoothness and simplicity of Jacob, while the latter should take care that they're not found to be harsh or cruel or twisted in their morals like Esau. Of those whose beards are in one, two, or three parts, the first should shun the solitary life and love the unity of peace, the second should preserve their conscience without neglecting their reputation, and the third should preserve the charity of *a pure heart, a good conscience, and an unfeigned faith,*[222] or with mind, hand, and tongue working together make their life harmonious. This style of beard was divided into three types above: on the chin or under the chin or on the jaws, or all at the same time. For those that have them, white beards should be *purer than snow, whiter than milk*, and red beards *ruddier than aged ivory;*[223] the soul of those with black beards should say: *I am black but beautiful.*[224] And because it is of a moderate color, those with a blond beard are subdued in their moderate charity, and are so ordinary and mild-mannered that they make themselves loveable to all and live among brothers without any quarrel.[225] Finally, those who have gray beards should be completely mature, like crops ready for the harvest, and brought to perfection in their virtues[226] should believe that the winnowing-fan and granary will soon be here.[227]

Chapter 41. *Some things about beards are only allegorical, others are both real and allegorical*

We must recognize, however, that in our readings about beards, some things are only allegorical while others are both real and allegorical. For example, when God makes a threat about the shaving of beards, it's only allegorical, since it doesn't seem believable that the beards of all the Assyrians were shaved, even though in the prophet it was said that among the Assyrians the Lord would shave *the entire beard.*[228] Likewise, when it was said that in Moab *every beard is shaved,*[229] we don't believe that any beard was shaved in accordance with this prophecy, because it was said only as an allegory. Furthermore, baldness must be understood in every case only as allegory, because just as among the Moabites no beard was shaved on account of the prophecy, there also wasn't baldness on any of their heads. However, what was said about beards turned out to be both real and allegorical in the case of Aaron's beard, David's beard, the beards of his servants, and perhaps Ezekiel's beard. What was said about the leprosy of the beard in Leviticus was only allegorical and not real, because no one's ever seen a leprous beard.

Chapter 42. *Four distinctions in the allegory of beards or other things*

Similarly, we must recognize that are there allegories of this sort not only in the case of beards, but in other things as well. In fact, there are allegories between one thing and another thing, between one action and another action, between a thing and an action, and between an action and a thing. Between one thing and another thing: beard and saliva, manna and vermin, shoot and flower, flower and fruit, tablets and the law. Between action and action: the work of Peter and the work of John, the struggle of Jacob and the struggle of the angel, the battle of David and the battle of Goliath, shaving the beard and burning, cutting, or scattering it. Between thing and action: a giant man and running,[230] a stag and a leap,[231] sheep and bathing,[232] beards and shaving, or the hairs of the beard and burning, cutting, or scattering them. When, however, an action is applied to a thing, as shaving to a beard, there's an allegorical relationship between the action and the thing, and so too when, conversely, a thing is applied to an action (or led or carried to it), as Isaac to the sacrifice,[233] Joseph to the sale,[234] sheep to the slaughter,[235] or hairs of the beard to burning, cutting or scattering, there's an allegorical relation between the thing and the action. Therefore, when what we read about beards is only allegorical, in the case of baldness combined with a beard we find that there's always a prophecy about the future from both of them. For example, *the Lord will shave the entire beard among the Assyrians* and *in Moab every beard will be shaved* are about the future, and in the same passage it was promised that in the future there would be *baldness on every head*.[236] Then in the same prophet there's the following: *The Lord will make bare the necks of the daughters of Zion and will strip them of their hair.*[237] And later: *And there will be baldness instead of flowing hair.*[238] This doesn't occur naturally nor did the outcome reveal any bald women, although we read that they did, albeit rarely, have beards, like Galla. But when what is read about beards is both real and allegorical, the narrative concerns the past, as is clear from the examples above.

Now as for the rest, brothers, because many things have been said about beards, collect in your thoughts what's to your benefit and keep fast in your memory what was said about the cleanliness of beards, their form, and their nature, and in all of this, let everything concerning allegory and morality serve both as a lesson to you in making your faith steadfast and as an adornment, graced with virtues, to your life and your vow.

Chapter 43. *Differences and similarities in tonsure and shaving between monks and lay-brothers*

Carefully review in your heart and your mind what I said about the similarities and differences between you and us in regard to shaving and the tonsure. We bring this up again, although you've already heard it, in order to add some other items you've not yet heard about. We perform three shavings and a have tonsure that you have in common with us, and you have one shaving that's in common with us. Therefore, we're the same in the two that are in the middle, while we differ in the two extremes, if in fact both we and you shave from temple to temple and are tonsured all around in a circle. Do you see then how the two intermediates, which are common to us and you, unite the extremes, in which we differ from one another because of their distinct forms? For we shave our beards and the top of our heads, but you shave neither your beards nor the top of your heads and in this you differ from us. We have, then, the four (that is, three shavings and one tonsure), and the middle two of these are common to us and you, but the two extremes are specifically assigned to us for shaving. For you, however, these extremes are allowed to be unshaven by the Order's Rule and the rationale for this Rule. But as the lower shaving in the case of our beards corresponds, as its opposite, to the lower preservation of your beards, so too does the higher shaving of our crowns coincide, as its contrary, with the hair on your higher part. And because there's too much dissimilarity and contrariety apparent in these extremities, two intermediates were found to give both us and you a similar appearance and to make the dissimilarity in the extremes seem somewhat less dissimilar. And in a way, the dissimilarity of the extremes is considered to be less dissimilar. For contraries could never be brought together to form a unity unless the contrariety of the contraries was modified by the interposition of intermediates. We remind you to carefully observe that the intermediates by which we are united in similarity are collaterals, or rather are conjointly connected.

Chapter 44. *That an O is formed by scissors and C by a razor and what these mean*

However, as these same things are formed by different instruments (scissors and razor), so too are these same things distinguished by their dissimilar form. For the razor is drawn from temple to temple to make a circle, but an incomplete one, while the tonsure in making its circuit completes the entire circle. The form of an incomplete circle produces the shape of the letter C, while the form of a complete circle produces the letter O. C is the third letter and second consonant. In its connection to the number three, because it's third, C signifies faith in the Trinity, which you and we possess equally, just as we and you have this shaving in common. The fact that C is the second of the consonants seems related to the shaving in this shape that's for both us and you, since with the first consonant [*muta*] we are commanded to refrain [*obmutescere*] from depraved speech, and with the second to remain silent even about good things on account of the dignity that comes from being taciturn; or C can also be called the second consonant because before taking the vow both we and you were completely mute in the confession of sins and in divine praise. According to the first interpretation, one could say: *I was mute and was humbled and I remained silent about good things,*[239] as if to say, "I was mute in depraved speech and in my humility I remained silent about good things." In the second interpretation, it could be said: *And I did not open my mouth,*[240] that is, "I was mute in confession and I did not open my mouth in divine praise."

The letter O is the fourth vowel, the thirteenth letter of the alphabet if H is not counted, the fourteenth if it is.[241] According to the first consideration, that it's the fourth vowel, both we and you are called from the four corners of the world and we ascend the chariot of Aminadab in the Gospel and we're all equally assigned to study the four virtues.[242]

As to the second consideration, according to which O is said to be the thirteenth or fourteenth letter, either we and you profess to imitate the way of life of the apostolic teachings, whose number is twelve and either Paul or Christ causes it to grow to thirteen; or we have sufficiently fulfilled the law and the gospel with the number ten and the number four.[243] Or, finally, if we follow the way of life mentioned, both we and you are assured of deserving the seven gifts of the holy spirit on the seventh day.[244] It's also worth noting that just as C is the first letter in the profession of our faith,[245] O is the second vowel in the declaration of divinity when it says: *I am the Alpha and the Omega.*[246] Each of the two letters illustrates the beginning of our conversion through Christ and the consummation of our perfection through the excellence of the divine majesty, the beginning as consummated, the consummation as confirmed. See how in the intermediates that unite us (the one shaving and the tonsure), even our differences, which are the extremes, are now judged to be less dissimilar. And because these are distinguished by certain levels, as it were, of the Order, we should continue to look into the meaning these differences and similarities have for us and you as well as for the Order's unity when no opposition splits it apart.

Chapter 45. *The meaning of shaving the beard and of shaving from temple to temple (that is, a templa in templam)*

Therefore, our first shaving in the beard lays bare, as it were, the chin [*mentum*] of our mind [*mentis*], so that through our education in doctrine we can reveal to ourselves wisdom, which we grasp with the mind, and thereby deserve to fulfil that promise of wisdom according to which it says: *Those who explain me will have eternal life.*[247] And because explaining wisdom through doctrine is our charge and doesn't concern you, we shave our beard, but you don't. But since we both shave from temple to temple, that is *a templa in templam*, let's examine what meaning this has for morals. The word for temples [*timpora*] is like the word for times [*tempora*] because it's recognized that they react to the times. Numerous blood vessels converge at the temples, and there's a great deal of movement and a palpable pulse; the movement or pulse is observed to be greater or lesser depending on whether the times are turbulent or calm. It's thus for good reason that the variability and movement in time's passing are exhibited in the temples, and based on them doctors often deliver their prognoses to the sick—whether their illness will afflict them more or less or whether they're going to die. Why else then do we shave from temple to temple, if not to remove the appetite and desire for temporal and mutable things, so that in shaving off the appetite, lust is shaved off, and in shaving off desire, greed is shaved off, the former a lust for acquiring, the latter a greed for things acquired? And because this is something that belongs equally to us and to you, this shaving is equally ours and yours. And since, if we exhibit this shaving, we can without a doubt expect a return of a hundred-fold, which C signifies, this shaving is given the shape of a C.

Chapter 46. *The meaning of the tonsure*

The tonsure, which removes part of the hair but also leaves a part, illustrates that in temporal matters the use of what's superfluous should be cut away, but it's permitted to retain the use of what's necessary. Don't you see that this applies equally to you and to us, just as the tonsure applies as much to you as it does to us? Indeed, the tonsure uncovers our eyes and ears, because the use of what's superfluous prevents us from hearing the word of God and equally obscures the eyes of the heart, and thus anyone who suffers from this can by no means say: *My eyes always to the Lord.*[248] It should also be noted that the circular course of the tonsure runs across the forehead to complete the O in order to show that there should be shame in the use of what's superfluous and that only by the use of what's necessary is it possible to reach Him who is the end of all, which the O illustrates by the perfection of its shape.

Chapter 47. *The difference between scissors and razor, given a two-fold moral interpretation*

We see there's still something else about the tonsure deserving our attention, namely that this form of monastic discipline, which is created with scissors, is recognized to be rather easy and pleasant to the same degree that the discipline performed with a razor is rather difficult and harsh. And who does not see how much easier and gentler it is to cut away the use of what's superfluous than to completely shave away from the heart the appetite and desire for temporal things? Something else seemingly pleasant to consider: why does a razor, having only a single blade, shave so roughly down to the root, but scissors, with two blades facing one another, remove not the whole but only a part? As it seems to me, in the words of our teaching and our Rule, there's something that cuts away everything harmful and damnable with a simple prohibition, like a razor, and there's something else that, with opposing statements coming together like scissors, suffices to cut away only what's superfluous. When someone says: *Do not love the world or the things in the world,*[249] it's like using a razor, but when someone says: *As having nothing yet possessing everything,*[250] it's like using scissors. You see how the two opposing blades of the scissors come together, as if to say *as having nothing* for the use of what's superfluous *yet possessing all* for the use of what's necessary.

Chapter 48. *That the allegory of the crown is common to monks and lay-brothers, or to clergy and laypeople, but the divine office is exclusive*

Finally, our shaving of the higher part enjoins upon us divine office, which distinguishes us from you, not because the allegory of the crown isn't common to us and you, but because in this shared allegory divine office is incumbent exclusively upon us. On the basis of this shared allegory, you'll possess together with us crowns for glory and honor in the blessed afterlife, but in this life we're marked out with the sign of the crown because we were chosen by lot for this particular office. For the office of the clergy, whose name, which is *cleros,* means "lot," requires this particular sign primarily to show by the bare top of our head that no other lot on earth intercedes between our lot and God. And because you're joined to our lot by your association with the Order, even though you don't have a crown like us as a mark of divine office, you will nevertheless have one like us when our rewards will correspond to our merits and both we and you will be crowned with glory and honor in that life of blessedness.

Chapter 49. *What it means that the bald have a tonsure as well as a shaving in the shape of a C, while those who aren't bald have a tonsure in the shape of an O and a shaving in the shape of a C.*

There's still another thing that seems necessary to address in regard to the tonsure (whose form in the shape of the letter O we've discussed), which isn't at all inapposite given the character of the tonsure. For those who are becoming bald, or rather who are completely bald, the tonsure turns out different. In their case, when scissors pass across the front of the head, they don't come across anything to cut, and so the O is changed into a C. As a result, the bald have a tonsure that's a C , like the shaving, while those who aren't bald have a tonsure that's an O and a shaving that's a C. It's worth asking what this means. If baldness is interpreted as a signifier of evil and a mark of ignominy, the O of the tonsure is changed into C when perfection slips into imperfection and ignominy succeeds glory. Thus the saying of Isaiah: *And instead of a sweet smell there will be a stench, and instead of a belt, a rope, and instead of curls of hair, baldness.*[251] But if baldness expresses the glory of the cross, because the place of Calvary is designated for the bald [*calvis*],[252] the change of the O into a C isn't bad, but good: it means to come from the perfection and fullness of virtues, which O signifies, to a reward of a hundred-fold, which C signifies. We see therefore that bald have a triple C (two from the razor, one from the scissors), while those who aren't bald have one C and a double O (a C and an O from the razor, and an O in the middle from the scissors).

Chapter 50. *What consideration should be given to the fact that neither a beard nor the shaving of the beard shows the form of any letter*

There's also the consideration that just as a beard doesn't have the shape of any letter, so too shaving the beard doesn't exhibit the shape of any letter. A beard is a marker of laical status and illiterate simplicity, and for this reason it's decreed for clergy that if anyone grows his hair or a beard, let him be an anathema.[253]

Chapter 51. *The three proportions among these four (the three shavings and one tonsure)*

In addition, we see three proportions among these four. The first proportion: the first is to the second as the third is to the fourth (with the order transposed). The second proportion: the first is to the third as the second is to the fourth (with the order transposed). The third proportion: the first is to the fourth as the second to the third (with the same order). In the first proportion, shaving the beard is for us and not for you and shaving from temple to temple is for us and for you, just as the tonsure is for us and for you and shaving the crown is for us and not for you. In the second proportion, shaving the beard is for us and not for you and the tonsure is for you and for us, just as shaving from temple to temple is for you and for us and shaving the crown is for us and not for you. In the third proportion, shaving the beard is for us and not for you and shaving the crown is for us and not for you, just as shaving from temple to temple is for you and for us and the tonsure is for us and for you.

Chapter 52. *What will become of beards and haircuts in the afterlife*

Not without reason do you ask, brothers, what will come of the various dissimilarities or similarities in shaving or tonsure in the next life—whether both we and you will either shave or not shave in the same way, or you will shave as you presently do, or we won't shave as we presently don't, or we will shave who currently don't, or you won't shave who currently do. I think we could truthfully reply that neither we nor you will shave or trim our beards or anything else there. What remains, then, is one alternative question, the second part of which can be treated separately and resolved: will we and you have beards there or will we remain beardless? As for the question of beardlessness, it will be the same as it is here, so that there too it will appear suitable only in the female sex. For as the Truth bears witness, in the masculine sex *not a hair from your head will perish*[254] and so neither will a hair from your beard. Nature won't be deprived of any of its honor and beauty in the hair, so neither will it in the beard. Indeed, in the next life there will be no baldness that nature doesn't restore to a complete head of hair, nor will there be any eunuchs, infants, or boys who won't end up with a beard which they would've had here or were going to have if they hadn't met with an early death or some accident hadn't inhibited their beards. But if the lack of a beard were somehow permitted to persist in men just as with women, it would still be less offensive to the senses of anyone who saw it than if women were to have beards like men. In fact, in the case of clergy or monks, it doesn't offend the eyes of their beholders if they've recently shaved, and as for women, it's nature that shows it's decent and appropriate for them to be without beards, while for men, on the other hand, the custom of shaving, acting like a second nature, makes them appear not unseemly when they have faces that are ex-bearded, just like the faces of women that are beardless by nature. However, since it fosters an even greater understanding of reason if nature maintains its law and order, in accordance with which in the next life as in this one men aren't without beards and women remain beardless, for the remainder let's consider the condition of beards in relation to that ultimate renewal.

It's worth asking, then, whether beard, hair, and nails, since they're superfluous to the body (which natural philosophers contend and holy men don't deny), are judged to be necessary in the next life. For nails as well as the hairs of the beard and on the head are said to be created from the continuous emanation and emission of humors, and frequent cutting of them proves they constantly grow. For even the beard of Arsenius,[255] which was extremely long from its constant growth, was said to have reached down to his belly, and certain hermits use their hair for cover in place of clothes. And so it happens that the whiskers of some men, when spread out, reach all the way back to the ears, and such men want to look wild and frightening, just like a boar of the forest looks wild and frightening with his large and horrible curved tusks.

Chapter 53. *What the condition of beards will be in the next life*

Will beards or other such things continue to grow in that life? Heavens no! For where there won't be frequent cutting, trimming or shaving, there won't be continuous growth. In fact, there will be a passing from the mobile and mutable to the fixed and stable, and glorified things will exist in an eternal state, with their mutable state giving way. The things which in this world *never remain in the same state*[256] will acquire in the next one a stable and fixed form in their eternal state. So it will be with beards—there they'll acquire a form such that they can be neither diminished nor increased, and the beard's form will be so completely becoming that they'll be perpetually clean, beautifully shaped, and in an inviolable natural condition. Because of their cleanliness they'll need no washing, no ointment or comb, and because of their eternal state, they won't fear any of the dangerous assaults that occur in this world, such as burning, plucking, or any thing of this sort.

Meanwhile, brothers, when you wash and comb your beards to make them clean, be careful you're not washing or combing a dog's hide rather than a human's beard. Beware the proverb "Wash and comb a dog, it's still the same dog," and also "You can't take the dog out of the dog with water or comb." In styling your beards, take care it's beauty is such that excessive attention to it doesn't make you vain and you don't become inflated with pride. In the nature of your beards, consider the maker who made them, so that, if there's anything in them you find distasteful, in criticizing what's distasteful you remain fearful of the sin of blasphemy against their creator. If someone comes to grief because of this, his beard will burn with great shame and a feeling of anguish, and though it doesn't feel cutting or burning here, there it will feel the worms and the flame.

Chapter 54. *Whose beards will be for punishment and whose for glory*

It's only fitting that whatever was the instrument of the sin be the source of its punishment, and that the instrument of iniquity should burn completely in the flame of Gehenna with a feeling of anguish. For many men, their beards were an instrument of pride, vanity, and lust, as was demonstrated well enough above. And as it is written: *Man is punished by the very things by which he sins.*[257] We know this happened in the case of the rich man's tongue which was tormented by flames,[258] and we have no doubt that the same thing happened to his beard. On the other hand, for those established in the kingdom of blessedness after the glory of resurrection, their beards, which they used in this life as a sign and instrument of piety and maturity, of wisdom and strength, and of their inner beauty, will be a source of happiness and joy and exultation. But woe to those weak and foul bearded ones, stupid and frivolous and irreligious, who strive to imitate neither girls nor beardless boys! This comes from the complaint of Saint Gregory: *What*, he said, *shall we who are bearded but weak say, when we see girls enter the celestial realms by the sword?*[259] Bearded and weak, he says, not bearded and strong—those whom anger overcomes, pride inflates, ambition agitates, luxury defiles. Therefore, to make sure the fact that we're bearded isn't turned to our shame should we be found to be bearded and weak, we should transform into a zeal for strength the contrary signs of weakness, so that after our beards are restored to a better state in the next life, then too will they bear witness to our glory there since we used them as an instrument for virtue here. But perhaps there are yet some who will say that in the glory of resurrection there's no need of any vaporous humors or any hairiness of head and beard, and that for the glory of heavenly joy it's good enough to be smooth like Jacob and not bristling with hair like Esau. But in response, it wasn't said that Jacob didn't have hair or a beard, but only that he was smooth and hairless in those parts where Esau, because of the corruption and viciousness of his nature, was bristling with hair beyond what's normal for other men. In fact, Jacob wouldn't have covered his hands and the bare part of his neck with goat skins unless he'd wanted to express the likeness of his brother Esau. This is why in this passage it says that his father *did not recognize him, because his hairy hands expressed the likeness of the elder brother.*[260] But why do we expend so much effort against those who raise their objections in vain, we who've received a promise about this from the creator of our hair and beards when he says to his martyrs (and also to us): *And not a hair from your head will perish?*[261] Nothing indeed can perish in that renewal, since martyrs have received from the Lord a promise about even their hairs remaining whole, and we've received it through them. And so also the saying of Saint Augustine: *Will a hand perish when a hair will not? Where not an eyebrow will perish will the eye?*[262] Thus we too say: does the beard perish when neither a hair from the head or body perishes? And so with this great promise *we await the Savior our lord Jesus Christ, who will reform the body of our lowness when it is made like to the body of his glory.*[263] When? When we will all enter together *into the unity of faith, to a perfected man, to the measure of an age of the fullness of Christ,*[264] and we receive the glory of our bodies in the wholeness of its parts and with the adornments of the hairs of the body, the hairs of the head, and the beard.

Chapter 55. *On the splendor and glory of beards in the next life*

What then will the splendor and glory of beards be? The same as hair's. In Revelation the hairs of the head appear white as wool, so won't beards also be white as wool?[265] If in that splendor and glory the *just man will shine as the sun*[266] or even be *whiter than snow* or *whiter than milk*,[267] how gleaming white do you think beards will be? When the just man shall *grow like the lily*[268] and flourish for eternity before the Lord, how will beards compare to these bright white lilies? And what will flourish for eternity before the Lord, will it be anything but the perpetual glory that resides in the adornments of hair and beards? When in his transfiguration Christ's face *will shine like the sun and his clothes will become white as snow*,[269] what is prefigured for us if not *the body of our humility transformed into the body of his glory*,[270] decorated with the hairs of the head and the beard as its adornments? If there was such great glory in the face of Moses that the sons of Israel couldn't look upon him for the splendor and glory of his face, which was removed,[271] how much brighter will the splendor and glory on our faces be, and how much more shining white will our beards be, which won't be removed? Therefore beards will not perish nor will they come to an end, at least not the end that is destruction, because they'll be perfected and consummated in the end that is consummation. And just as the recognition of truth will shine in the miraculous clarification and glorification of our faces, our beards, because they occupy the greater part of the face, will be a great support to our understanding, so that as soon as someone's beard becomes visible, there can be no doubt about his beard's <splendor and glory>.[272]

Notes

1 A coinage by Burchard, punning on the terms for beard (*barba*) and barbarous *(barbarus)*. The words were not in fact etymologically related, but the use of (pseudo-) etymological connections was common since antiquity and was a favorite tool of biblical exegesis. Burchard uses the method several times in this work.

2. Anathema can refer to the ritual used to formalize excommunication, but at times was treated as something distinct and more severe: excommunication was separation from the church, anathema was condemnation to hell. However, anathema is often used in the general sense of a curse. See E. Vodola, *Excommunication in the Middle Ages* (Berkeley: Univ. of California Press, 1986) 14-16, 46-7.

3. Refers to an earlier letter now lost.

4. Perhaps from Psalm 65 (66):12: *transivimus per ignem et aquam*. The phrase is often taken to refer to the fires of purgatory.

5. Isaiah 9:5

6. Reading *quia* with the manuscript instead of *qui* printed by Huygens.

7. Psalm 132 (133):2. The Latin of the biblical text is *in barbam, barbam Aaron*, which is usually translated as "the beard, the beard of Aaron." Burchard, perhaps playfully, interprets the phrase as a doublet ("the beard-beard of Aaron"), which he explains in chapter 4 of this sermon.

8. The three types of vermin Burchard names (*lentipedes, lendes, pediculi*) seem to be kinds of lice, and there are three kinds of lice known to infest humans (the body louse, the head louse, and the crab louse).

9. The name of this vermin is *pediculus* (the modern Linnaean classification for lice). Although the first half of the name derives from the Latin for foot (*pes*), the latter half is related to the Latin for eye (*oculus*) in appearance only. Burchard explains the significance of the name in the next chapter.

10. 1 Timothy 1:5

11. Psalm 39:5 (40:4)

12. James 1:8

13. Psalm 24 (25):15

14. 1 Timothy 1:5

15. Leviticus 13:29

16. Leviticus 13:30

17. Jeremiah 4:22

18. Leviticus 13:31-34

19. The seven-fold Spirit (*septiformis spiritus*), a concept dating to the third century AD, refers to the seven gifts of the spirits mentioned at Isaiah11:2.

20. Leviticus 13:51-52

21. Matthew 8.4; Luke 5:14

22. Leviticus 13:57

23. Isaiah 9:5

24. 1 Samuel 21:10-15

25. Psalm 21:7 (22:6)

26. 2 Corinthians 11:19

27. 2 Corinthians 11:20

28. 1 Corinthians 1:25

29. Isaiah 9:5

30. Sapientia (Wisdom) 5:3-6. A phrase from verse 6 ("the sun has not risen for us") has been inserted between verses 4 and 5, with *sol intelligentiae* ("the sun of understanding") becoming simply *sol.*

31. The name Achish is etymologized as if from the Hebrew words for "how" and "to be." Jerome, however, interprets the name to mean "my brother" or "brother man"; see P. De Lagarde, ed. *Liber interpretationis Hebraicorum nominum.* Corpus Christianorum 72 (Turnholt: Brepols, 1959) 102. The passage beginning with this sentence and continuing until "like his beard, was hidden within" in the next chapter is dependent upon Rabanus Maurus' commentary on the books of Kings (*In libros Regum,* see Migne, *Patrologiae Latinae* 109.60Aff.). Rabanus (ca. 780-856 AD) was a Benedictine monk who became archbishop of Mainz but is better known as an intellectual who wrote numerous treatises and commentaries.

32. 1 Corinthians 1:22-25

33. See DuCange 1.610, s.v. *bavosus,* which he defines as *stultus* (stupid).

34. Job 7:19

35. Job 2:8

36. *grennones.* See DuCange 4.100, s.v. *grani.*

37. It is not clear exactly what the "military style" is. "Curials" are inhabitants of a city who met a minimum wealth requirement and thus served as public

officials who carried out civic functions, often at their own expense.

38. Isaiah 41:15

39. 2 Samuel 10:4-5

40. The passage following the quotation is heavily dependent on Rabanus Maurus' commentary on Kings; see note 31.

41. According to Jerome; see P. De Lagarde, ed. *Liber interpretationis Hebraicorum nominum.* Corpus Christianorum 72 (Turnholt: Brepols, 1959) 137, 157.

42. Isaiah 7:20

43. Amos 3:6

44. Isaiah 15:2

45. 2 Corinthians 3:16

46. The crown refers to the tonsure.

47. On the "old man" and "new man," see Ephesians 4:22-24.

48. Ezekiel 5:1

49. Ezekiel 5:1-4; Burchard omits a couple of phrases.

50. Psalm 35:7

51. Psalm 77 (78):49

52. Isaiah 9:5

53. Psalm 20:10 (21:9)

54. Isaiah 66:24

55. Ephesians 6:17

56. Galatians 5:12

57. Psalm 88:24

58. 1 Corinthians 5:13

59. Psalm 11:9 (12:8)

60. Revelation 22:15

61. Psalm 132 (133):1

62. Psalm 132 (133):2

63. Psalm 1:4

64. *gyrovagus* is a compound word meaning "wandering in circles." See the Rule of St. Benedict 1.10-11: "The fourth kind of monk is called the gyrovague. His entire life is spent in different regions, staying as a guest for three of four

days in the cells of different monasteries, always wandering and never settled, a slave to his own pleasures and his gullet's delight, and in all ways worse than the Sarabaites." (Sarabaites are the third kind of monk, criticized for their undisciplined way of life dedicated to gratifying their own pleasures.)

65. Isaiah 15:2

66. Job 1:20

67. The existence of Saint Alexis is doubtful, but he was supposed to have lived in the fifth century AD. See *Acta Sanctorum*, July 17, 4.253 C (vol. 31).

68. Justina converted Cyprian to Christianity, and both were tortured and killed in 304 AD during the emperor Diocletian's persecutions of Christianity.

69. *Acta Sanctorum*, Sept. 26, 7.201 A (vol. 47)

70. Simeon Stylites the Elder, fifth century AD. See *Acta Sanctorum*, Jan. 5, 1.268, ch. 8.28 (vol. 1).

71. *Acta Sanctorum*, Aug. 25, 5.34 D-E, ch. 1.4 (vol. 39)

72. The questions are based on 1 Corinthians 9:5, Luke 6:1, and Matthew 15:20.

73. Ecclesiastes 3:1

74. *Acta Sanctorum*, August 25, 5.37 E, ch. 2.19 (vol. 39)

75. Isaiah 61:3

76. 2 Kings 2:13; Ruth 3:9; Isaiah 28:20

77. Matthew 20:16, 22:14

78. Matthew 10:22

79. Galatians 5:6, with the substitution of *dilectionem* for *caritatem*.

80. Luke 12:49, with *ardeat* in place of *accendatur*.

81. Isaiah 64:1-2

82. Deuteronomy 4:24, Hebrews 12:29

83. Ezekiel 20:16

84. Ezekiel 5:8-10

85. Psalm 118:96

86. John 6:61

87. Psalm 20:3 (21:2)

88. John 13:27

89. Isaiah 9:5

90. Zachariah 8:19

91. Know "in the biblical sense," i.e. have sex with them.

92. Gregory the Great, *Dialogues* 4.14.1-2. See A. de Vogüé, ed. *Grégoire le Grand: Dialogues, Tome III: Livre IV* (Paris: Éditions du CERF, 1980) 54-6; O.J. Zimmerman, trans. *Saint Gregory the Great: Dialogues* (Washington, DC: The Catholic University of America Press, 1959) 205-06.

93. Burchard introduced both examples, from 2 Samuel 10:4-5, at Sermon 2.2.

94. Gregory the Great, *Dialogues* 4.14.2. See A. de Vogüé, ed. *Grégoire le Grand: Dialogues, Tome III: Livre IV* (Paris: Éditions du CERF, 1980) 56; O.J. Zimmerman, trans. *Saint Gregory the Great: Dialogues* (Washington, DC: The Catholic University of America Press, 1959) 206.

95. In Proverbs 8:20-33, Wisdom (*sapientia*) is personified and "preaches" on a street corner. Since the Latin noun is grammatically feminine in gender, personified Wisdom is a female deity. The capitalization of Wisdom is a modern convention to indicate the personification.

96. Proverbs 8:29-31

97. Genesis 18:10-12

98. In biblical Hebrew, the name Isaac does mean "laughter." See Genesis 21:3-6; and Jerome in P. De Lagarde, ed. *Liber interpretationis Hebraicorum nominum.* Corpus Christianorum 72 (Turnholt: Brepols, 1959) 67, 136, 152, 155, 157.

99. 2 Kings 2:23

100. 2 Corinthians 5:13

101. Job 5:6

102. See Leviticus 16:18-21.

103. 1 Corinthians 1:20

104. Genesis 1:26

105. Romans 8:7

106. Leviticus 16:5-19

107. The phrase is often used by Augustine; see Huygens (1985) 182 for references.

108. Genesis 27:5-10

109. 1 Peter 2:21-22

110. Leviticus 16:10, 21-22

111. John 18:40, Luke 23:18, Matthew 27:21

112. 1 Timothy 3:16

113. Deuteronomy 32:14

114. Proverbs 5:3

115. *Ars Poetica* 161-162

116. Matthew 23:3. For the symbolism of the jaw (*maxilla*), see Jerome, *Ep.* 64.2: "The jaw symbolizes an eloquent and educated man, so that we speak with our mouth what we believe in our heart." In A. Hilberg, ed. *Epistularum Pars I: Epistulae I-LXX*. Corpus Scriptorum Ecclesiasticorum Latinorum 54, 2nd ed. (Vienna: Verlag der Österreichischen Akademie der Wissenschaften, 1996) 589.

117. 2 Corinthians 5:13

118. Psalm 55 (56):12

119. Psalm 65 (66):13-14

120. Psalm 65 (66):15

121. Psalm 65 (66):15

122. Galatians 5:24

123. Romans 15:4

124. Acts 10:13, with *macta* for *occide*.

125. Isaiah 58:7

126. Isaiah 21:14

127. Lamentations 4:4

128. A conflation of Ezekiel 34:8 and Jeremiah 23:1.

129. Psalm 126 (127):2, 77 (78):25. Barley bread (*panis [h]ordeaceus*) was coarse bread, and is the bread used for the miracle of loaves and fishes (John 6:9).

130. 1 Kings 19:4-8

131. Judges 15:15-16

132. Genesis 49:14

133. Luke 6:29

134. Isaiah 9:5

135. Mentioned in chapter 4 of this sermon.

136. Boethius, *Consolation of Philosophy* 1.1.11

137. Psalm 70:18

138. See 3 John 9: "I had written to the church, but Diotrephes, who likes to behave as if he's first among them, did not welcome us." For Jerome's interpretation of the name, see P. De Lagarde, ed. *Liber interpretationis Hebraicorum nominum.* Corpus Christianorum 72 (Turnholt: Brepols, 1959) 151.

139. Proverbs 26:7

140. 2 Samuel 9:13

141. 2 Samuel 19:24

142. From Jerome, see P. De Lagarde, ed. *Liber interpretationis Hebraicorum nominum.* Corpus Christianorum 72 (Turnholt: Brepols, 1959) 108.

143. 1 Paralipomenon (1 Chronicles) 8:34 and 9:40

144. Romans 13:2

145. 2 Samuel 19:25-26

146. Exodus 16:20

147. Leviticus 14:9

148. Leviticus 19:26-27

149. Sirach (Ecclesiasticus) 10:15

150. Sedulius, *Paschal Song,* pref. 3

151. Romans 8:9

152. Romans 12:2

153. This chapter is taken from Augustine's *Enarrationes in Psalmos* ("Expositions on the Psalms") 132.7-9, with some omissions and alterations. D.E. Dekkers and J. Fraipont, eds. *Enarrationes in Psalmos CI-CL.* Corpus Christianorum 40 (Turnout: Brepols, 1956) 1931-32; M. Boulding, trans. *Saint Augustine: Expositions of the Psalms.* Vol. 6. (Hyde Park, NY: New City Press, 2001).

154. Acts 7:51

155. Acts 7:60

156. Ephesians 5:27

157. Galatians 6:2

158. Romans 11:20

159. Romans 12:3

160. Job 15:26. "Armed with a fat neck" in the Latin Vulgate is the result of a misunderstanding; the complete verse in the original Hebrew is "he charges against him with a stiff neck, with the thick bosses of his shield."

161. Goldschmidt suggests a possible allusion to Abelard's *Sic et non*.

162. Matthew 5:34-36

163. *Epistola Luciani* 2 (Migne, *Patrologiae Latinae* 41.809). *geroprepes* is from the Greek ἱεροπρεπής ("fit for something holy").

164. 1 Timothy 2.7

165. *Epistola Luciani* 3 (Migne, *Patrologiae Latinae* 41.809)

166. Job 12:12

167. Wisdom of Solomon 4:8

168. Psalm 89 (90):12

169. Daniel 13:52, a later addition to the Hebrew text and thus not found in many bible translations.

170. Wisdom of Solomon 4:8-9

171. A *dalmatica*, a liturgical garment worn by bishops.

172. John the Deacon, *Vita Gregorii Magni* 4.83 (Migne, *Patrologiae Latinae* 75.229B). John describes paintings Gregory had placed in the monastery of S. Andrea in Rome, still visible in his day. In the atrium were two paintings: one of his father Gordian being received by a seated Saint Peter, the other of his mother Silvia. A third painting, in a small apse (*absidula*) behind the storeroom, was of Gregory himself, which Burchard refers to below. See G. B. Ladner, *I ritratti dei papi nell' antichità e nel medioevo* (Rome: Pontificio Istituto di Archeologia Cristiana, 1941) I.70.

173. Sermon 2.1.

174. John the Deacon, *Vita Gregorii Magni* 4.84 (Migne, *Patrologiae Latinae* 75.230B)

175. *in rota gypsea*. Probably a fresco, perhaps an *imago clipeata*; see G. B. Ladner, *I ritratti dei papi nell' antichità e nel medioevo* (Rome: Pontificio Istituto di Archeologia Cristiana, 1941) I.72.

176. Ephesians 3:17

177. Ezra 9:3

178. Ezra 9:3 (quoted in full below)

179. The remainder of this paragraph is taken from Bede's commentary on Ezra. See D. Hurst, ed. *In Ezram et Neemiam*, Corpus Christianorum 119A (Turnout: Brepols, 1969) 327-8; S. DeGregorio, trans. *Bede: On Ezra and Nehemiah* (Liverpool: Liverpool University Press, 2006) 139-40.

180. Matthew 22:1-14

181. 1 Samuel 1:11

182. Luke 21:18

183. Leviticus 14:8-9. See chapter 17 of this sermon.

184. i.e., Ezra. "Priest" translates *pontifex*; Bede may have thought at one time that Ezra held the office of high priest among the Jews or he may have simply used to term in a general sense for a religious leader. See S. DeGregorio, trans. *Bede: On Ezra and Nehemiah* (Liverpool: Liverpool University Press, 2006) 113n7.

185. Macarius was an Egyptian ascetic of the fourth century AD and an important figure in the early history of monasticism. Fifty homilies were attributed to him, but not until the twentieth century was the attribution proven to be false. Burchard uses *abbas* ("abbot"), which is found in the text he cites. Macarius would have been called *abba* ("father") as a sign of respect, but he did not hold the office of abbot. Burchard, however, might have considered him to be one. Vindemius is not otherwise known, and the name may derive from a Coptic original; like Macarius, he was not an abbot. For Macarius, see W. Harmless, *Desert Christians: An Introduction to the Literature of Early Monasticism* (Oxford: Oxford University Press, 2004) 194-6.

186. *Vitae Patrum: Verba Seniorum* 6.3.2 (Migne, *Patrologiae Latinae* 73.1004C-D). Scetis was a monastic settlement founded by Macarius in the desert west of the Nile delta, in Wadi al-Natrun, and became a major center of early monasticism.

187. 2 Samuel 20:9

188. Josephus, *Antiquities of the Jews* 7.11.7. Burchard apparently had access to a Latin translation.

189. 2 Samuel 20:9-10

190. For the interpretation that follows, see Gregory the Great, *Moralia in Job* 15.13 in M. Adriaen, ed. Corpus Christianorum 143A (Turnholt: Brepols, 1999), 756; B. Kerns, trans. Gregory the Great: *Moral Reflections on the Book of Job*. Vol. 3. Collegeville, MN: Liturgical Press, 2016). Also Rabanus Maurus, *In libros Regum* (Migne, *Patrologiae Latinae* 109.112B).

191. Luke 2:52

192. Vergil, *Aeneid* 9.251

193. This chapter lists only seven types.

194. Psalm 72 (73):9

195. Mark 10:47

196. Ephesians 6:17

197. Psalm 118 (119):140

198. Perhaps a reference to Romans 9:21

199. Psalm 38:4 (39:3)

200. Psalm 72 (73):21

201. 2 Corinthians 4:7

202. Job 12:5

203. Luke 15:8-9

204. Ecclesiastes 4:12

205. A combination of Psalm 135 (136):5 and Joshua 8:35. Burchard seems to take *intactum*, normally translated as "untouched," in the sense of "unbroken."

206. Genesis 1:14-18

207. Micah 6:8

208. Psalm 33:2 (34:1)

209. Matthew 22:37, Mark 12:30, Luke 10:27

210. Isaiah 15:2. See Sermon II.4.

211. See Sermon II.7.

212. See chapter 5 of this sermon.

213. *Vitae Patrum: Verba Seniorum* V.15.10 (Migne, *Patrologiae Latinae* 73.955B). For Gordian's beard, see Sermon III.22.

214. Genesis 25:25, 27:11

215. 2 Samuel 20:9-10; Josephus, *Antiquities of the Jews* 7.11.7. See chapter 27 of this sermon.

216. See chapter 34 of this sermon.

217. Proverbs 1:26

218. 2 Kings 2:23. See chapter 8 of this sermon.

219. Genesis 32:24-32

220. 1 Samuel 16:12

221. Romans 11:33

222. 1 Timothy 1:5

223. Lamentations 4:7

224. Song of Solomon 1:4

225. Philippians 3:6

226. Wisdom of Solomon 12:17

227. Matthew 3:12

228. Isaiah 7:20. The Latin for "entire," *universus*, could also taken in a collective sense.

229. Isaiah 15:2

230. Psalm 18 (19):6

231. Isaiah 35:6

232. Song of Solomon 6:5

233. Genesis 22:2-10

234. Genesis 37:27-28

235. Isaiah 53:7

236. Isaiah 7:20, 15:2

237. Isaiah 3:17

238. Isaiah 3:24

239. Psalm 39 (38):3

240. Psalm 39:10

241. The letter H, as an aspiration that was not always pronounced, was not always counted as a letter. Also, the letters I and J are not counted as separate letters in Latin.

242. For the chariot of Aminadab, see Song of Solomon 6:11. The four classical virtues are *fortitudo* (courage, strength), *temperantia* (temperance, moderation, self-control), *prudentia* (prudence, wisdom), and *iustitia* (justice).

243. The ten commandments and the four gospels.

244. For the seven gifts, see Isaiah 11:2-3.

245. i.e., *credo in unum deum* ("I believe in one God").

246. Revelations 1:8

247. Sirach (Ecclesiasticus) 24:30 (Vulgate)

248. Psalm 24 (25):15

249. 1 John 2:15

250. 2 Corinthians 6:10

251. Isaiah 3:24

252. The association of Calvary with baldness was sometimes attributed to the shaving of Jesus' head before his crucifixion.

253. Burchard seems also to have the eighth century "Gregorian" decree in mind: *si quis ex clericis relaxaverit comam, anathema sit* ("If any member of the clergy grows his hair long, let him be an anathema."). See Constable (1985) 103-8.

254. Acts 27:34

255. Arsenius was tutor of the sons of the emperor Theodosius before becoming a hermit in the Egyptian desert around 395 AD. For long beard, see *Acta Sanctorum,* July 19, 4.628B (vol. 31).

256. Job 14:2

257. Wisdom of Solomon 11:17

258. Luke 16:19-25

259. Gregory the Great, *Homiliae in evangelia* I.11.3 (R. Étaix, ed. Corpus Christianorum 141. Turnholt: Brepols, 1999. 75). See also D. Hurst, trans. *Forty Gospel Homilies.* (Piscataway, NJ: Gorgias Press, 1990) 64. (Homily 9 in his renumbering of the first twenty homilies).

260. Genesis 27:23

261. Acts 27:34

262. Sermon 31.2.2 (Migne, *Patrologiae Latinae* 38.193)

263. Philippians 3:20-21

264. Ephesians 4:13

265. Revelation 1.14

266. Matthew 13:43

267. Lamentations 4:7

268. Hosea 14.6 (said of Israel)

269. Matthew 17:2

270. Philippians 3:20-21

271. 2 Corinthians 3:7

272. The manuscript breaks off, but it is clear the sermon is drawing to a close. Huygens supplied these last words based on the heading of this chapter.